Bitches,

Bimbos

and

Ballbreakers:

The

Guerrilla

Girls'

Illustrated

Guide

to

Female

Stereotypes

Penguin Books

Bitches, Bimbos and Ballbreakers:
The Guerrilla Girls' Illustrated Guide to Female Stereotypes

by the Guerrilla Girls

This book is dedicated to our supporters all over the world.
We can't thank you enough for your inspiration, and your stories.

PENGUIN BOOKS
Published by the Penguin Group
Penguin Group (USA) Inc., 375 Hudson Street,
New York, New York 10014, U.S.A.
Penguin Group (Canada), 10 Alcorn Avenue, Toronto, Ontario, Canada M4V 3B2
(a division of Pearson Penguin Canada Inc.)
Penguin Books Ltd, 80 Strand,
London WC2R 0RL, England
Penguin Ireland, 25 St Stephen's Green, Dublin 2, Ireland
(a division of Penguin Books Ltd)
Penguin Group (Australia), 250 Camberwell Road, Camberwell,
Victoria 3124, Australia (a division of Pearson Australia Group Pty Ltd)
Penguin Books India Pvt Ltd, 11 Community Centre, Panchsheel Park,
New Delhi - 110 017, India
Penguin Books (NZ), cnr Airborne and Rosedale Roads, Albany,
Auckland, New Zealand (a division of Pearson New Zealand Ltd)
Penguin Books (South Africa) (Pty) Ltd, 24 Sturdee Avenue,
Rosebank, Johannesburg 2196, South Africa

Penguin Books Ltd, Registered Offices:
80 Strand, London WC2R 0RL, England

First published in Penguin Books 2003

10 9 8 7 6

LIBRARY OF CONGRESS CATALOGING IN PUBLICATION DATA
Bitches, bimbos, and ballbreakers : the Guerrilla Girls' illustrated guide to female
    stereotypes / by the Guerrilla Girls.
        p. cm.
    ISBN 0 14 20.0101 5
    1. Women—Psychology. 2. Stereotype (Psychology) I. Guerrilla Girls (Group of artists)
    HQ1206.B444 2003
    305.4—dc21   2003051749

Printed in the United States of America
Written and Designed by the Guerrilla Girls Frida Kahlo and Kathe Kollwitz

Previous books by the authors:
Confessions of the Guerrilla Girls
The Guerrilla Girls' Bedside Companion to the History of Western Art

Contents

CHORWOMAN AUNT JEMIMA BALLBREAKER BIKER CHICK BIMBO BITCH BOMBSHELL BRA BURNER BULL DYKE BUTCH CALL GIRL CARMEN MIRAN

- A STEREOTYPE
- IS A BOX,
- USUALLY
- TOO SMALL,
- THAT A GIRL GETS
- JAMMED INTO.

Chapter **One**

WHATEVER LIFE A WOMAN LEADS, FROM BIKER CHICK TO SOCIETY girl, there's a stereotype she'll have to live down, or live up to. What have you been called? Daddy's Girl? Bull Dyke? Dumb Blonde? Feminazi? Are female stereotypes based on universal truths? Are they overactive fantasies piled on top of one another? Why does our culture produce so many categories for women? (We dare you to come up with half as many for men.)

Introduction
What's in a name?

  The Oxford English Dictionary (OED) defines "stereotype" as a simplified conception or idea that gets invested with special meaning by a certain group of people. An archetype is slightly different: It's a model or an ideal from which duplicates are made.

  Think of it this way: A stereotype is a box, usually too small, that a girl gets jammed into. An archetype is a pedestal, usually too high, that she gets lifted up onto. Some archetypes can be stereotypes, like a Mother Teresa or even a Bombshell. But there are lots of stereotypes that would never be considered archetypes: Trophy Wife, Bitch, Gold Digger, etc. Stereotype or archetype, it's rarely a girl's own choice: It's a label someone else gives you

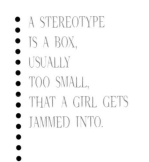

A DOLL COCKTEASER DADDY'S GIRL DEBUTANTE DIVA DOMINATRIX DRAGON LADY DUMB BLONDE DYKE FAG HAG FEMME FEMME FATALE

From one Britney Spears, many.
© Reuters NewMedia/Corbis

Who needs cloning when we have stereotypes?

to make you less or more than you really are.

Some stereotypes are positive (The Girl Next Door, Prostitute with a Heart of Gold), but many more are pejorative (Old Maid, Jewish-American Princess, Welfare Queen). Lots of them reduce a woman to a sex object or insult her by implying she's a prostitute (Wench, Slut).

There are stereotypes that grow out of religious myth. The Virgin/Whore dichotomy evolved from the contrast between the Virgin Mary and Mary Magdalene during the life of Christ. Lilith, the Bitch Goddess, was Adam's first wife. She demanded equality, got kicked out of paradise, and was replaced by Eve.

Other stereotypes are rooted in the exemplary lives of real women, like Florence Nightingale, or in the tragic lives of others, like Marilyn Monroe, the embodiment of the Dumb Blonde/Blonde Bombshell. Some are invented to sell products (Aunt Jemima). Some, like Lolita and Vamp, were conjured up by poets and novelists. Others have mutated over time. Broad and Ho, for example, used to refer to prostitutes, but later came to refer to any female of the species.

Stereotypes are living organisms, subject to laws of cultural evolution: They are born, they grow, they die and/or change to fit the times. They have an umbilical connection to language: They gestate in popular culture and are born in everyday slang.

The most prolific progenitor of stereotypes today is the media: movies, TV, music, newspapers, and magazines. Media-specific stereotypes leap across borders and cultures with terrific ease. For instance, young girls today in every part of the world and in every ethnic or economic substrata imaginable get bombarded via TV and the Internet with the Rock Starlet stereotype: a thin, young, long-haired (usually

• Marilyn
• Monroe: Was
• she a Bimbo or
• did she just act
• like one?

© Bettmann/Corbis

EMINAZI FLAPPER GEISHA GIRL NEXT DOOR GOLD DIGGER GOOD CATHOLIC GIRL HAREM GIRL HO HOMEGIRL HOT TAMALE INDIAN PRINCESS JEWISH PRI

blonde) woman with her shirt way down to there to show her cleavage and way up to there to bare her midriff, grinding into a phallic microphone. Stereotypes like this have great power. In fact, psychologists are convinced that the projection of stereotypes leads to stereotyped behavior. For years the belief that girls were inherently

A 1995 STUDY FOUND THAT THREE MINUTES A DAY SPENT LOOKING AT A FASHION MAGAZINE CAUSED 70 PERCENT OF WOMEN TO FEEL DEPRESSED, GUILTY, AND SHAMEFUL.

Beauty and its beasts

A 12-year-old Guerrilla Girl fan recently wrote us, "I've noticed something very strange about those oh-so-lovable fairy tales, such as *Cinderella, Snow White,* and *Sleeping Beauty.* Whenever the main character is female, her greatness always depends on how beautiful and fair she is, and on her ladylikeness and meekness. Any female in these fairy tales who has any power at all must be ugly or evil...or both. I think this is horrible." The tyranny of beauty has determined women's lives throughout the ages, reappearing in different generations and cultures in ever more oppressive and unattainable body images.

Today, the most popular beauty stereotype is the ultrathin model, described in magazines as "pencil slim," "cigarette slim," or using other sticklike metaphors. This ideal has thrown millions of females into despair, self-hatred, and even anorexia and bulimia. In Western culture, over the last few hundred years, the ideal woman has become skinnier and skinnier. As recently as the 1980s, models were 8 percent thinner than the average woman; today they're 23 percent thinner. In the days when few could afford the amount of food needed to get there, fat used to be considered the epitome of female beauty. Now, the higher her social class, the more likely a woman is to starve herself to thinness.

So what will be next in the beauty pantheon? One thing's for sure, whatever beauty stereotype is in our future, we'll spend far too much time trying to attain it, most of us with little success. The Guerrilla Girls believe it's great to look your best, but if women could only cut in half the time we spend making ourselves look good (and chastising ourselves for not looking good enough) we could take over the world. Then, we could pass a law: no more impossible notions of beauty.

AVERAGE WOMAN

MODEL

> **Broad and Ho used to refer to prostitutes but came to refer (often affectionately) to any female.**

inferior at math trickled down to a shockingly small number of women confident enough to enter careers in science. If this Rock Starlet stereotype persists, the Guerrilla Girls think it could make human cloning irrelevant. Many of us will be virtual clones already.

Which brings us to why we decided to write this book in the first place: We want to mitigate the power of female stereotypes over our lives. In the following pages we will investigate the origins, histories, and namesakes of some of the most beloved and the most notorious female stereotypes of our time. By taking a closer look and poking holes in some auras, we will praise the good ones, take back some of the negative ones, and propose ways to escape them if we want.

Every stereotype has a history or at least a few good stories behind it. We will begin by considering the top stereotypes, the ones that follow us from cradle to grave, from Tomboy to Old Hag. Then we'll take a spin through some of the stereotypes that surround all the varieties of our sexual selves. After that we will go behind the lives of real and fictional women who have become stereotypes. Some invented their own stereotype (Carmen Miranda), some had it thrust upon them (Tokyo Rose). We'll also look at occupational stereotypes, from Soccer Mom to Female Exec.

Our examination of stereotypes could not be complete without the ones that describe women from specific ethnic and religious groups. These were so insulting we had to make fun of them by creating our own collection of ethnic stereotype dolls.

In our final chapter we'll offer a few ideas that you can use to fight stereotyping in your life.

By empowering women to create their own stereotypes and to reject the ones our culture tries to squeeze us into, the Guerrilla Girls want to do our share toward saving the world from sexists and misogynists everywhere, and have fun along the way.

Chapter Two

THE FIRST TIME WE GET STEREOTYPED IS IN UTERO. EVER BEEN invited to a baby shower where the baby's sex is unknown? You try to buy a gender-neutral gift only to find that almost everything manufactured for infants is gender coded—right down to diapers and safety pins!

From cradle to grave:
The top stereotypes

Even though all infants do pretty much the same things—eat, sleep, cry, and fill their pants—from their first day they do so identified as a male or a female. Baby girls wear clothes adorned with pink hearts to let them know that all they really need is love. Baby boys are dressed in blue with patterns of fire engines and trucks to prepare them for the manly careers that lie ahead. Without these gender signifiers, it's almost impossible to know if a clothed baby is male or female.

We're used to this pink-for-girls, blue-for-boys thing, but before about 1920 boys and girls under the age of four or five were dressed almost alike. They both had the same curly locks and wore frilly lace dresses. It was pretty hard to tell them apart.

Then, in the early 20th century, a group of social reformers, some of them women, campaigned for clothing to become more functional and decided that boys and girls ought to be dressed differently, starting at birth. They sug-

Can you tell the gender of the Victorian-era baby below?

One-year-old boy, 1902. BT Batsford Ltd, London

Y'S GIRL TOMBOY GIRL NEXT DOOR BIMBO FEMME FATALE/VAMP BITCH/BALLBREAKER GOOD/BAD MOTHER SPINSTER/OLD MAID HAG/CRONE

gested color coding: pink for boys and blue for girls. Over time it somehow got switched. Why did gender-specific colors catch on, after years of babies being dressed identically? Was it the fear and unease fomented by the women's suffrage movement? Was it an attempt to validate Freud's theory that "anatomy is destiny"? Was it to prepare boys for the world wars? For whatever reason, over the course of the 20th century, as adult clothing became more and more unisex (blue jeans, T-shirts, sneakers), infant wear became more and more gendered.

Why is being a Daddy's Girl a good thing but a Mama's Boy a bad thing?

• • • • • • • • • • • •

A girl begins her life decked out in stereotypical fashion: hearts and flowers, ruffles and lace. As she grows, stereotypes will confront her at every stage of life. Here are some of the most persistent, the ones that define her from cradle to grave, from Daddy's Little Girl all the way to Old Hag.

Daddy's Girl

A Daddy's Girl is the apple of her father's eye. And she's proud of it! Daddy is so wonderful and important, and she is so special to receive his attention. Being a Daddy's Girl is a good thing. A 1977 study of women executives found that all of them had an especially close relationship with their fathers, much closer than with their mothers.

Being a Mama's Boy, on the other hand, is a bad thing. A Mama's Boy is suffocated and emasculated by too much maternal affection. The mother of a Mama's Boy is a self-centered, needy shrew who manipulates her male child into overdependency. (See "The Mother of All Stereotypes," page 27.)

On the surface, the idea of a Daddy's Girl is

© The Norman Rockwell Family Entities

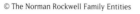

innocent. But scratch the veneer and all sorts of forbidden meanings, obsessions, even sexual implications emerge. Do an Internet search for "Daddy's Girl," and up come hundreds of porno sites displaying underage girls. In the 1930s, Cole Porter wrote "My Heart Belongs to Daddy." We're not sure whether the song refers to an actual father or to a lover. Marilyn Monroe called her husband Joe DiMaggio "Daddy"; thousands of American wives do the same. Then there were the Sugar Daddies from Sugar Hill in Harlem—older, wealthy African-American men who bankrolled elegant lifestyles for their younger mistresses in exchange for sex.

Freud believed that daughters overly attached to their fathers are also hostile to their mothers and suffer from an "Electra Complex." He got the idea from a grossly dysfunctional family in Greek mythology. Agamemnon sacrificed his daughter, Iphigenia, to the Gods to win the Trojan War. Incensed, his wife, Clytemnestra, took a lover and together they murdered Agamemnon. A second daughter, Electra, with brother Orestes, killed both mother and lover to avenge their father. Electra is the Xtreme Daddy's Girl. Freud saw hints of eroticism and sexual jealousy buried in her connection to Daddy and her hatred of Mom. Was Freud right? Is a Daddy's Girl always in competition with her mother? Is there a sexual component in the intense attachment between a Daddy and his Little Girl?

Which brings us back to the Daddy's Girl/Mama's Boy dichotomy. The same culture that celebrates the affection between a father and daughter ridicules the loving involvement of a mother with her son. Is this a backhanded approval of male privilege? Is it some kind of unconscious acceptance of the history of father-daughter sexual abuse? In an age when sexual abuse by parents is no longer a dirty family secret, what are we to make of the Daddy's Girl with its many shades of interpretation? The Guerrilla Girls believe a new term is needed to describe the healthy affection of a father for a daughter. And while we're at it, let's rehabilitate the Mama's Boy, too, and invent a brand-new stereotype to describe the positive influence of a mother's love on her male children.

COLE PORTER'S "MY HEART BELONGS TO DADDY"

While tearing off a game of golf,
I may make a play for the caddy.
But when I do, I don't follow through
'Cause my heart belongs to Daddy.

If I invite a boy some night
To dine on some fine finnan haddie,
I just adore his asking for more
But my heart belongs to Daddy.

Yes my heart belongs to Daddy
So I simply couldn't be bad,
Yes my heart belongs to Daddy
Da da da, da da da, da da da.

I want to warn you laddie,
Though I think you're perfectly swell
That my heart belongs to Daddy,
'Cause my Daddy, he treats me so well!

MARY MARTIN

'My ♥ Belongs To Daddy'

with
Bing Crosby
Eddy Duchin
Jack Teagarden
Woody Herman

including
Let's Do It
I Get a Kick Out of You
Foolish Heart
What Is This Thing
Called Love?
The Waiter, The Porter
and the Upstairs Maid

HER CAREER BELONGS TO DADDY?
Wherever I go, most of the women executives I meet between 30 and 50 tell the same story. They say they had successful, supportive fathers who were the ones to tell them to go out there and get 'em.
—John Davis, Harvard Business School

13

Tomboy

Norman Rockwell called his 1953 painting of a tomboy (above) *Triumph in Defeat*. The GGs are disappointed in him: Why didn't he think of her as having WON the fight?

The Tomboy wasn't always a girl. The term's long history dates back to the 16th century when it was used to describe a young guy who drank too much and carried on with wenches. By the 19th century, the naughty label was bequeathed to the opposite sex and came to mean a rude, crude, immodest woman—a slut. By the 20th century, "Tomboy" was a label for a physically active girl who liked to do the same physical things as a boy—in other words, a jock.

At a time when girls were expected to stick around the house and learn to cook, clean, and sew, a girl who liked sports was thought of as unfeminine. Guerrilla Girls see it a little differently. Girls who were Tomboys took a look around and saw boys had all the luck: They could run, jump, play sports, and express themselves physically. These girls ignored what was expected of them and joined in the fun! They didn't necessarily want to be biological boys, they just wanted to do what boys always had the freedom to do.

A Tomboy was amusing and accepted, but at puberty she was expected to "grow out of it" and become ladylike. If she didn't, and kept up her boyish behavior as an adult, well then, maybe she was...homosexual. Many a parent feared that a Tomboy daughter might grow up to be a Lesbian. Female gym teachers were always suspect.

In the early 20th century, America had a celebrity Tomboy: Mildred "Babe" Didrikson. Born in 1911, Babe excelled in sports from an early age. Not just one or two, but every one she tried: basketball, baseball, tennis, track, acrobatics, swimming, skating, squash, and billiards. In the 1932 Olympics she qualified for five events but was allowed to compete in only three. She set records in each. In a world where women athletes couldn't make a living, Babe was forced to cash in on her celebrity status by playing football in publicity films and starring in a vaudeville routine driving golf balls into the audience from a treadmill while singing. Finally, she devised a way to become one of the first professional women

SPORTS

BABE IS A LADY NOW

The world's most amazing athlete has learned to wear nylons and cook for her huge husband

Mildred Babe Didrikson, whose middle name really is Babe, was once designated by Grantland Rice as "the athletic phenomenon of all time, man or woman." Certainly no athlete, man or woman, ever approached Miss Didrikson's versatility. Gertrude Ederle, first woman to swim the English Channel, was often called the greatest feminine athlete who ever lived, but this seems a singularly ill-considered

"WHAT A BABE!"
Texas tomboy is first U.S. woman to win British golf championship

As everyone knew she would, the able Mildred Didrikson Zaharias last week won the British women's amateur golf championship. Only once did she falter. That was on the last day of the tournament, when the tomboy from Port Arthur, Texas tried to be a lady and wore a skirt. The Babe grimly charged back to her dirty but lucky blue-corduroy pants and drove her opponent off the blue-swept Firth of Forth course. Said a dismayed wind-swept Firth of Forth...

Babe gets feminine in *Life* magazine, June 23, 1947.

AMERICA'S MOST ENDURING TOMBOY

Jo March was the independent Tomboy sister in Louisa May Alcott's *Little Women* **(1869). She complained about wearing skirts and even went outside in the winter and threw snowballs, which was pretty daring for that time. The book was loosely based on Alcott's real family, with herself as the model for Jo. Millions of fans, even today, identify with Jo's boyish behavior and her ambition to become a writer—to do more with her life than just marry.**

Of course, the fictional Jo does eventually get hitched and leave her Tomboy days behind. She falls for an older man, they have kids (all male), and run a boys' school together. In real life, Alcott neither married nor had children.

golfers: She started the LPGA tour.

Babe was butch. Asked by a reporter if there was anything she didn't play, she said, "Yeah, dolls." When a female spectator questioned her gender by shouting, "Where are your whiskers?" Babe fired back, "I'm sittin' on 'em sister, just like you!" *Long* before Muhammad Ali, she proclaimed herself not just good, but "the greatest."

Babe's Tomboy image was way too strong for the time. Rumors circulated that she was a Lesbian, and she received lots of negative press. One reporter said that her accomplishments "merely demonstrated that in athletics women didn't belong, and it would be much better if she and her ilk stayed home, got themselves prettied up, and waited for the phone to ring." To keep her career on track, Babe took his advice and became outwardly feminine. She got a new hairdo and put on flowery dresses and makeup. She married a pro wrestler and told reporters the most thrilling night of her life was the first time she had sex with him. That was the public Babe. The private Babe formed a close friendship with a young female golfer who moved in with her and her husband. It has long been alleged, but never confirmed, that they were lovers.

Today, female athletes are celebrated as never before, but the old stereotypes about them haven't completely disappeared. They're still expected to act as feminine and

THINK TIMES HAVE CHANGED SINCE BABE DIDRIKSON WAS TOLD TO BE MORE FEMININE? Here's what Martina Navratilova said in 1998: "I don't know why they have the women dolled up in these skin-tight outfits. I mean, if that's what they really think it takes to attract an audience, why not just send them out there naked? You don't see them primping the men players. Why is it so necessary for women athletes to prove themselves as women?"

Top to bottom: Martina Navratilova (©Dimitri Lundt, TempSport/Corbis); Anna Kournikova (©Duomo/Corbis); Serena and Venus Williams (©Reuters NewMedia/Corbis)

I smile a lot, I win a lot, and I'm really sexy. —Serena Williams

• Homegirl:
• The Girl
• Next Door
• when
• home is
• the hood.
•
•
•

heterosexual as possible. Look at the erotic costumes worn by female figure skaters. And why is it that female gymnasts compete bare-legged while male gymnasts wear pants?

Female athletes who don't care about makeup or clothes or who are Lesbian and open about it are rarely featured in the media. When Martina Navratilova was the top tennis player of all time, she got very few commercial endorsements. Was this due to her muscular physique and her sexual orientation? Today, tennis champions Venus and Serena Williams are power athletes with even more muscle development than Martina ever had, but they enjoy wearing sexy little cutout dresses, elaborate hairstyles, jewelry, and a lot of makeup. And they make tens of millions in endorsements! Anna Kournikova, a tennis babe of the white, blonde variety, makes big bucks in endorsements and can be seen half naked on lots of magazine covers, even though she rarely wins tournaments.

Why is the world of professional sports afraid of gayness? Guerrilla Girls demand that Eternal Tomboys, those women athletes who remain boyish all their lives and sleep with whomever they choose, not be swept under the carpet by a media obsessed by mainstream hetero ideas of what is feminine.

The Girl Next Door

The Girl Next Door

Parents who can't wait for their Tomboy to "grow out of it" probably hope that when she does, she'll evolve into one of the most feminine stereotypes: the Girl Next Door. According to the *OED*,

NOT the Girl Next Door

GNDs, clockwise from top: Doris Day, Marie Osmond, Sandra Bullock, Julia Roberts, Reese Witherspoon, Donna Reed, Grace Kelly

Not GNDs, clockwise from top: Bette Davis, Mae West, Courtney Love, Angelina Jolie, Lucy Liu, Madonna, Joan Crawford, Jayne Mansfield

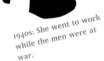

1940s: She went to work while the men were at war.

1950s: She began to go to college in large numbers.

1960s-1970s: The sexual revolution made it okay for her to have premarital sex. The birth control pill and abortion rights made pregnancy a choice. The gay liberation movement made it easier for her to be openly Lesbian.

1970s-1990s: With better wages and personal freedom through women's lib, she didn't have to live at home anymore.

she's a "trusting, sweet, faithful but unimaginative woman." She is the familiar, the unexotic, the undifferent, a mirror of conventional family values. She's almost always white. The Girl Next Door is pure, loyal, and would never think to question authority. She's straight out of a Norman Rockwell painting. She's Doris Day, Marie Osmond, Sandra Bullock, Julia Roberts. She's NOT Mae West, Marilyn Monroe, Madonna, or Lucy Liu.

Central to the idea of the Girl Next Door is the message that no matter how far men roam and what exciting lives they lead, when it comes to mating, they come right back to where they started. The Girl Next Door stayed home because it was the best place in the world to be.

Of course, one reason the Girl Next Door stayed home is that for a long time women weren't allowed to go anywhere. Until the last half of the 20th century, most good girls didn't leave home to go to school or to work. Even those who were educated or had jobs lived at home until they got married and assumed the career they had been raised for: homemaking and motherhood. When a rare female adventurer took off alone to make her fortune in a big city, her reputation became suspect.

Until the 1960s the Girl Next Door was attractive and desirable, but she didn't put out. She was supposed to remain a virgin until engaged, if not married, to Mr. Right. If she couldn't wait, the Girl Next Door became the Slut Down the Block.

Then times changed. Women fought for the right to higher-paying jobs that used to be open only to men. They rented their own apartments, lived alone, and started to do as they pleased. Today, the Girl Next Door goes on her own adventures. In fact, she no longer

> I suggested that sex was not the enemy...that nice girls have sex. The centerfold itself, the girl next door centerfold... was rooted in that philosophy.
> —Hugh Hefner

Hugh Hefner with some of his "Girls Next Door," 2001
© Rufus F. Folkks/Corbis

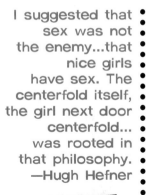

Y'S GIRL TOMBOY GIRL NEXT DOOR BIMBO FEMME FATALE/VAMP BITCH/BALLBREAKER GOOD/BAD MOTHER SPINSTER/OLD MAID HAG/CRONE

waits around for a lot of things, including sex. Britney Spears might have started out a homespun Mouseketeer Next Door, but she quickly grew up into a midriff-baring teen sexpot/mogul.

How did the Girl Next Door get a sex life? Did an income of her own trigger her libido? Was it the pill that changed her? Woodstock? Feminism? *Playboy?*

Hugh Hefner, founder of *Playboy,* has always claimed that the Playmates in his magazine—blonde (no pubic hair, please), big breasted, and ready for wholesome sex—are Girls Next Door. This was revolutionary in the 1950s. Before *Playboy,* only bad girls posed naked. Today, Girls Next Door from all over the country flock to L.A. to take off their clothes for Hugh. Their parents are often proud of them for it! They remain the Girl Next Door because they are still trying to please the Boy Next Door.

The Girl Next Door may have morphed into an educated, working, sexual being, but she isn't an endangered species. She still stands for what most men still want in a woman: sweetness, obsequiousness, loyalty, and a good piece of you know what!

A 1987 film, Full Moon Pictures/Tempe Entertainment

Bimbo/Dumb Blonde

"Bimbo" started out gender neutral—from the Italian word "bambino" (baby)—and became progressively female. In the flapper era, a Bimbo was a terrific person of either sex. By the 1930s, detective novels made a Bimbo the opposite: a dope, a bozo, either male or female. Somewhere between the Second World War and the 1960s, a Bimbo became exclusively female: usually a beautiful, curvaceous blonde (Monica Lewinsky notwithstanding) with tight clothes, high heels, and a not-so-high IQ.

In the mid-1980s, the media became obsessed with the illicit female sexual companions of famous men. One after another of these women—from Donna Rice to Jessica Hahn to Gennifer Flowers—were canonized as Bimbos in the press. The Bimbo stereotype was born!

Today's Bimbo is a young, ambitious woman who has sex with an older, powerful man in order to become famous or self-important. She's babelicious with big tits and sexy

OKAY, WE COULDN'T RESIST JUST ONE DUMB BLONDE JOKE, BUT IT'S SORT OF A FEMINIST BLONDE JOKE:

A blind man orders a drink at a bar and says to the bartender, "Hey, you wanna hear a blonde joke?" The bar immediately becomes absolutely quiet. In a husky, deep voice, the woman next to him says, "Before you tell that joke, you should know something. The bartender is blonde, the bouncer is blonde, and I'm a 6-foot-tall, 200-pound blonde with a black belt in karate. What's more, the woman sitting next to me is blonde, and she's a weight lifter. The lady to your right is a blonde, and she's a pro wrestler. Think about it seriously, Mister. You still wanna tell that joke?" The blind guy thinks a moment and says, "Nah, not if I'm gonna have to explain it five times."

clothes, and she's so gullible she does and believes everything he says. She also happens to be white.

Variations on Bimbodom have emerged, too: Bimbette (a very young Bimbo), Jumbo Bimbo (stewardess who is a Bimbo), Bimbo eruptions (Bill Clinton's sexual escapades), Bimbo control (the job of keeping the former to a minimum), etc. Then, of course, there are the male counterparts: Himbo and Hunk.

Bimbos prove the tiresome, sexist assumption that women can't have both beauty and brains. Men and other women feel superior to a Bimbo because they assume she's dumb. Unlike the scheming Vamp (see page 20), a Bimbo is easily dominated and usually humiliated.

Men want to date Bimbos, but no woman wants to be called one. It's hard to find actresses who admit to being Bimbos, but it's

Are they really Bimbos or do they just pretend to be?
Top row, from left to right: Marilyn Monroe
(© Bettmann/Corbis); Judy Holiday (© John Springer
Collection/Corbis); Jayne Mansfield; Barbie.
Bottom row, from left to right: Pamela Anderson (© Corbis);
Carmen Electra (© Reuters NewMedia/Corbis);
Anna Nicole Smith (© Bettmann/Corbis);
Monica Lewinsky (© Rufus F. Folkks/Corbis)

MEGIRL BITCH BIMBO FEMME FATALE VAMP GOOD MOTHER BAD MOTHER WICKED STEPMOTHER SPINSTER OLD MAID HAG CRONE TOMBOY

easy to find them playing Bimbos in movies or on TV. They have little choice: Nuanced, intelligent roles for women are few and far between. Actresses like Pamela Anderson play up their Bimboness looking gorgeous, acting stupid, and laughing all the way to the bank.

To women, a man with a Bimbo on his arm (a Bimbo hound) is considered shallow, afraid of smart women and "real relationships." Among men, he's envied for attracting such awesome "arm candy."

These Bimbo girlfriends never gain weight, never get old, never ask questions, never get tired of sex, and never tell. If he's married and they get caught, or if he dumps her, she gets her chance to step out of the stereotype, write a book, go on a lecture circuit, and make a lot of money, showing she isn't such a Dumb Blonde after all.

Lilith by John Collier, Akinson Art Gallery, Southport, England

Femme Fatale/Vamp

The Femme Fatale is an evil, conniving woman hell-bent on seducing men and leading them to ruin and damnation. Sometimes she does it for material gain, sometimes just for thrills. Men find her irresistible and are reduced to helpless prey in her cunning clutches. If there were really as many of these evil women out there as history and culture say, it's a wonder there are any guys left standing.

The truth is that Femme Fatales slink through the ages mostly in fiction, not in fact. Almost all are the creation of imaginative male minds who believe their own sexual urges can't be controlled and, if things get out of hand, it's gotta be someone else's fault. These guys also insist there are legions of Femme Fatales out there, just waiting to destroy them. Femme Fatales are everywhere in art, theater, movies, literature, and religious myth. A film wouldn't be noir without one.

Here are a few of these evil girls: In the beginning there was Eve, who got us all thrown out of paradise. Then there was Delilah, who seduced Samson and reduced him to a wimp with a simple haircut. And let's not forget Salome, who performed her lurid Dance of the Seven Veils then took as payment the head of John the Baptist on a silver platter.

The Greeks gave us the Sirens, whose singing lured sailors to their deaths. The temptress Circe turned Odysseus's fighting men into swine. Helen of Troy's beauty launched a thousand ships and ignited the Trojan War. What power these women exercised with only their sexual allure! With skills like these, we women should have taken over the world centuries ago!

One can certainly argue for the existence of a few real-life Femme Fatales, but their destructive impulses are usually exaggerated in the literature they inspired. Was Cleopatra, Queen of Egypt, a seductress extraordinaire, or an astute but tragic military and political leader simply doing what Egyptian convention dictated: commingling her sex life with political power? Required by custom to marry her brother then cede power to him, she seduced Julius Caesar who helped her regain her throne. He got himself assassinated in the process. Forced to marry a second brother, she took up with another Roman, Marc Antony, and used his armies to protect her power. But she and Antony ended up at war with the rest of Rome. He killed himself when he thought she had died. She killed herself to avoid being captured. Cleopatra was hardly a triumphing Femme Fatale although she is often remembered as one.

Closer to our own time, 19th-century art and literature are littered with manipulating seductresses and victimized men. In 1887, Philip Burne-Jones did a

Edvard Munch showed his fear of the sexuality of Vamp(ire)s in this 1895 lithograph. Eric Lessing/Art Resource, NY.

painting he titled *The Vampire*, to get back at a married actress who dumped him. His cousin, the poet Rudyard Kipling, wrote an accompanying poem with the same title, about the evils of this particular woman and, by extension, all women who spurn men. What a family act, reducing noncompliant women to bloodsucking vampires! The poem was transformed into a play, and the play into an early silent film, *A Fool There Was* (1915). This film started a craze for Vamps, shortened from "vampire," and made a star of actress Theda Bara, who went on to play Vamp after Vamp in early silent films.

In *A Fool There Was*, Bara plays a Femme Fatale with a notch on her belt for each man brought to his doom. She plots to seduce an upstanding society man, the happy husband of a loyal and virtuous wife and the adoring father of a beautiful little girl. Unable to control himself, he leaves wife and child, slavishly following the Vamp to the ends of the earth, becoming a wasted shadow of his former self. He's the pathetic victim, she the supernatural she-devil.

The film is Victorian: sentimentality is glorified; marriage, motherhood, and family are all sacred. Female sexuality is treacherous and wicked. Turning away from the values of hearth and home leads directly to debauchery and damnation.

But the Vamp in *A Fool There Was* triumphs and the moral system fails, mirroring the anxieties of early-20th-century society where a culture war was raging. While convention told women their place was at home with their husbands and families, suffragists were pressuring for the vote and on the verge of getting it. Flappers were waiting in the wings ready to tell women to take off their corsets and raise their skirts (see page 59). Both sides of this social conflict found validation in the idea of the Vamp. Traditionalists could boo and jeer the evil, man-eating aspect of the New Woman. Modernists could thrill at her cool vengeance upon centuries of male domination.

This version of the Vamp soon went out of fashion, but something of the original Vamp got passed down from generation to generation, mutating in the process. After Theda Bara came Pola Negri, Anna May Wong (see sidebar, left), Marlene Dietrich, Greta Garbo, Bette Davis, and Joan Crawford.

More recently, Catherine Deneuve and Susan Sarandon went all the way as Lesbian Vamp(ire)s in *The Hunger* and Sharon Stone put a bisexual twist on the Vamp in *Basic Instinct*. B movies are filled

How the lady became a Vamp

In the early days of films, studios created a celluloid persona for an actor and expected her to be in character 24/7. Theda Bara, born Theodosia Goodman, was happily married to writer/director Charles Brabin all her life. But in public she presented the studio fantasy of herself as a Vamp and never discussed her private life. She got typecast and her subsequent films included *The Devil's Daughter, Sin, The Galley Slave, Destruction, The Serpent, Gold and the Woman, The Eternal Sappho, The Vixen, The Tiger Woman, Cleopatra, Salome, When a Woman Sins, The She-Devil, Siren's Song,* and *Madame Mystery.* Need we say more? In the end she was frustrated by this stereotyping. She made 40 movies in five years and then her career was pretty much over.

The vampire I play is the vengeance of my sex upon its exploiters. You see, I have the face of a vampire, perhaps, but the heart of a *feministe.* —Theda Bara
quoted in *Virgins, Vamps, and Flappers* by Sumiko Higashi

Theda Bara photos courtesy Pam Keesey

Sharon Stone and Grace Jones.
Photos courtesy Pam Keesey

with Vamp themes and more Lesbian vampires. Grace Jones appeared as the vampire Katrina in *Vamp* (1988) and released a concurrent CD titled *Love Bites*.

In 1987, Glenn Close played a version of a Vamp in the movie *Fatal Attraction*. Unlike Bara, who triumphs in the original Vamp plot, Close and her unborn child end up dead in the bathtub, killed by the conventional Good Wife to cheers from the audience.

By acknowledging only our sexual power, the Femme Fatale stereotype denies us other forms of power. It also pits women against each other, because at any moment a Vamp might be after your partner, who will be powerless to resist.

THE CAMP VAMPS: OVER-THE-TOP PERFORMERS WHO ACTED OUT THE VAMP STEREOTYPE

In the 1950s, chorus girl Maila Nurmi showed up at a Halloween Ball done up as Vampira, an outrageously sexy vampire. That got her a gig as the late-night announcer of horror films, *The Vampira Show*. She kept up this schtick offstage, driving around L.A. in a Packard with a chauffeur, emitting blood-curdling screams at intersections. In the 1980s, Cassandra Peterson, a gorgeous Vegas showgirl, morphed herself into Elvira, the cult goddess of the film *Mistress of the Dark,* half vampire, half material girl. She hosted horror shows, promoted products like Coors beer, became a permanent character at an L.A. theme park, hosted a TV special, and declared herself a candidate for the presidency in 1992. "The voters keep putting boobs in office," she said, "so they might as well be mine." Which brings us to Vampirella, a sweet comic-book vampire from outer space unable to adapt to eating habits on planet Earth. She fights her blood lust like a dieter counting calories and kills humans only when desperate, and then with great remorse.

Left to right: *Vampire's Night Orgy.*
Elvira, Vampirella
Photos courtesy Pam Keesey

Bitch/ Ballbreaker

Call a woman a Bitch or a Ballbreaker and what image comes to mind? A strong, aggressive female who isn't afraid to speak her mind, suffers no fools, and takes no nonsense. Not bad personality traits. So why does a Bitch strike terror in the hearts of men? Why does a woman take offense when called a Bitch? Is it less of an insult when a girl uses it to describe another girl? How about when she uses it to describe herself? Here's a look at the stereotype and the growing culture of bad girls who have begun to celebrate it.

"Bitch" is a slang term with a long history. In Middle English, circa 1000, a bitch was a female dog and still is. But around 1600 it began to be used to describe a brazen, unpleasant, selfish, lewd woman, the opposite of the loyal, instinctively selfless, fiercely protective domestic female dog. Current usage of the word goes back and forth between the animal that can be controlled (female dog, prostitute) and the animal that can't (the willful woman). It's also meant a lot of other things over the years.

How do we love to use the word "bitch"? Let us count the ways. There's a bitch (a difficult thing); to bitch (to complain); to bitch up (to ruin); to bitch off (to make angry); bitchy (spiteful); bitching (violent, mean); bitchin' n' twichin' (great). Then the combos: Stone Bitch (a woman who cannot be moved); bitch party (a woman's tea party); Bitch Booby (a country girl); bitch's wine (champagne); bitch session (a gathering to air grievances); the Rich Bitch (a wealthy and difficult woman); the Bitch Goddess (a successful or a powerful woman in history); a Bitch in Heat (an impatient, impulsive, sexually aggressive woman). Finally, there's the queen of slurs, which takes its power from a derogatory reference to a guy's mother, the Son of a Bitch (see the top of page 29). Confusion over the acceptable use of "Bitch"

Covers from *Bitch*, one of our favorite magazines and part of the bitch-empowerment movement

The difference between a Bitch and a Slut is that a Slut is someone who sleeps with everyone and a Bitch is someone who sleeps with everyone but you. —Internet joke

I'm tough, ambitious, and I know exactly what I want. If that makes me a Bitch, okay. —Madonna

Madonna © Reuters NewMedia/Corbis

DY'S GIRL TOMBOY GIRL NEXT DOOR BIMBO FEMME FATALE/VAMP BITCH/BALLBREAKER GOOD/BAD MOTHER SPINSTER/OLD MAID HAG/CRONE

Supermodel Naomi Campbell
©B.D.V./Corbis

abounds. One noted linguist thinks it's such an insult that we should stop using it to describe female dogs! Contemporary street culture plays fast and loose with the word "bitch," using it so often it has come to mean not a difficult woman but any female at all, and often any man who deserves to be belittled. The BBC Standards Commission recently ruled that it was okay for a comedian to call the Queen of England a Bitch on air because the word is no longer offensive, it just means any woman. In a 1995 survey of men and women in the U.S., 93 percent of the respondents felt it was "very inappropriate" for men to refer to women they don't know as Bitches. (What about women they do know?) Another survey the same year produced a different result: Fewer than half the participants felt Newt Gingrich should apologize to Hillary Rodham Clinton for calling her a Bitch. What's a girl to think?

Obviously, Bitch is a stereotype in transition. A developing culture of unrepentant Bitches can be found everywhere! There's *Bitch* magazine; there's a growing industry of Bitch-empowerment books. If the world is going to call you a Bitch for being ambitious, outspoken, and in control of your own sexuality, why not accept it and be proud? If we use it to describe ourselves, it can't be used against us. We say, "Bitches of the world unite." Be tough, get what you want, be a real Bitch. But don't let anyone else call you one!

Senator Hillary Rodham Clinton
© AFP/Corbis

The Mother of All Stereotypes:
Good or Bad, Sainted or Smothering

Who can make a grown man cry? His mother. Who can make him regress to a frightened infant? Mom again. When she's good, she's very, very good (the Blessed Mother, Mother Teresa), but when she's bad she's horrid (Medusa, Livia Soprano).

For every kind of mother, there's a stereotype to fit. Here are just a few: Good Mother, Bad Mother, Mother from Hell, Blessed Mother, Suffocating Mother, Castrating Mother, Controlling Mother, Devouring Mother, Pushy Mom, Good-Enough Mom, Supermom, Earth Mother, Suffering Mother, Barefoot Mother, Fairy Godmother, Hot Mama, Jewish Mother, Mother Hen, Welfare Mother, Mother-in-Law, Single Mom, Soccer Mom (see page 77), and Stage Mom (page 78).

Madonna Litta, Leonardo da Vinci, 1490-91. Hermitage State Museum, St. Petersburg, Russia

67 percent of Americans call their mothers every day

THE YUMMY MUMMY

There was a 1980s children's cereal character called the Yummy Mummy, but that's not what we're talking about here. We're talking Jada Pinkett Smith. We're talking Reese Witherspoon. We're talking babes who have babes. A Yummy Mummy is sexy even while she's pregnant. And after the baby is born, she instantly fits into her prepregnancy clothes—miniskirts and bikinis included. She wouldn't be caught dead in muumuus or baggy sweats. She's the opposite of the tired, trapped, unkempt housewife who spends long hours serving her husband and kids and never has time for herself. How does the Yummy Mummy do it? She has a full-time nanny, a personal trainer, and LOTS of money, honey. How else?

Jada Pinkett Smith © Corbis

TURKEY, MICRONESIA, HAITI:
FUCK YOUR MOTHER

FRANCE:
SON OF A WHORE

ETHIOPIA, ARMENIA,
BULGARIA, BURMA, SUDAN, SENEGAL:
I WILL FUCK YOUR MOTHER

U.S.:
MOTHERFUCKER

CHINA:
I WILL FUCK YOUR MOTHER'S
BROKEN-DOWN STINKING CUNT

In many cultures, insulting a persons' mother is akin to a declaration of war (see above). In the U.S., there's also a jokey insult game (Your mama's so ugly that...).

Then there's the use of mother to mean something very important: Mother Nature, Mothership, Mother England, Mother of Invention, Mother of All Battles, Mother Tongue, Motherland, Mother Lode, Motherboard, Mother Church, Mother Superior. The mentor of a group of drag queens is known as the Mother.

She's patient, always upbeat, and completely understanding. Her kids respect her. She never raises her voice. She exists only to pack a nutritious lunch and maybe crack a few jokes. She's Donna Reed, Carol Brady, Florida Evans, more recently, Clair Huxtable and Debra Barone. And, of course, there was Morticia Adams, the perfect mom if your family was truly weird.

THE SITCOM MOM

Even today, when less than 12 percent of women are stay-at-home moms, a TV mom is likely to be one. The quintessential sitcom mom was June Cleaver, played by Barbara Billingsley on *Leave it to Beaver* from 1957 to 1963. She was loving, unfailingly nice, always deferrred to her husband, and never yelled at the Beave no matter what kind of trouble he got into. What made those sitcom moms so perfect when our own moms were so flawed? Hint: They had writers!

Above: Barbara Billingsley as June Cleaver.

ITALY:
ON OF A SOW

LAOS:
YOUR MOTHER FUCKS DOGS

SPAIN:
I SHIT IN THE MILK OF YOUR MOTHER

ENGLAND:
SON OF A BITCH

ROMANIA:
I FUCK YOU IN THE ASS ON YOUR MOTHER

NEW GUINEA:
YOU EAT YOUR MOTHER'S MENSTRUAL BLOOD

We love our mothers and hate them—and spend years on the couch talking about them. Mother stereotypes are big-time because motherhood is a BIG job, one of the most important. We could try to level the playing field and demand more stereotypes for fathers. But the Guerrilla Girls don't want to do battle with mothers or fathers. They have a hard enough time bringing up kids as individuals in a culture bent on reducing everyone to mindless stereotypes!

THE WICKED STEPMOTHER

Mothers can and do mistreat their children, but we hate to think of them as being anything but sweet and loving. Enter the Wicked Stepmother. In fairy tales, according to psychologist Bruno Bettelheim, she functions as a surrogate for the unacceptable feelings of hostility and fear that children have for their mothers, real or step. Were there always Wicked Stepmothers or did they get their bad rap from all those fairy tales? Well, there are certainly stepmothers who resent their stepdaughters' youth and beauty. And there are stepmothers who privilege their biological kids over their stepkids. But most stepmothers try to do a good job; it's often the stepchildren who won't let them. "I tried and tried, but I couldn't get the kids to accept me" is a common refrain among stepmoms.

Above: Your basic fairy tale wicked stepmother.

> Spinsters are
> man-condemning,
> man-hating...women
> who are independent
> of men, a motley
> host, pathetic in their
> defiance of the first
> principle of Nature
> but of no serious
> account in the
> biological or social
> sense. —*Modern
> Woman and How
> to Handle Her*,
> a 19th-century
> self-help book

Spinster/Old Maid

An unmarried woman is sad, lonely, pathetic, frumpy, and sexually repressed. No, wait, that was in the olden days. Today an unmarried woman is sad, lonely, pathetic, adorable, and sexy—like Ally McBeal, Bridget Jones, and the *Sex and the City* girls.

"Old Maid" is an American term, popularized by the eponymous children's card game. "Spinster" is the British term. Both are derogatory. So why do even left-leaning publications in the U.K. like *The Independent, The Guardian,* and *The Times* refer to unmarried women as Spinsters—and especially when said Spinsters are victims of murder, robbery, or sex crimes?

Why is a woman's lack of a husband so important to note? And why is our collective image of an Old Maid/Spinster so negative? This is one stereotype the Guerrilla Girls are intent on turning inside out and upside down.

Headlines from British tabloids

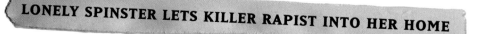

LONELY SPINSTER LETS KILLER RAPIST INTO HER HOME

Accused Denies Murdering Spinster in "Sexual Frenzy"

A Cautionary Tale of Two Spinsters

Evicted Spinster to Return Home After Anonymous Donor Comes to Her Rescue

TRAGIC END FOR SPINSTER

For centuries, a woman was the property of the men in her family. If she didn't have a husband, she remained the charge of a next-of-kin male: father, brother, uncle. She wasn't legally allowed to own property, run a business, sign a contract, or inherit money. To make things worse, a girl's family had to offer a dowry as an incen-

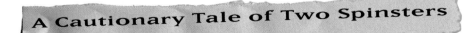

tive to a prospective husband. Less-than-wealthy families squandered what little they had on an advantageous marriage for one daughter, leaving other daughters penniless and unmarriageable.

It doesn't take a genius to realize that in those days, a woman's most important job in life was to find a husband—the most financially secure one that her looks and/or family income could attract. And she was working against her own biological clock: Once she was no longer young and beautiful, no man would want her. A Spinster or Old Maid was the woman who failed this crucial task and could look forward to a life of confinement in the house of a relative, or maybe in a nunnery. 19th-century novelists,

especially Jane Austen, wrote about the unfairness and terror of this period in a woman's life.

An additional punishment heaped on a Spinster was celibacy. Until recently, it was assumed that unmarried women who weren't prostitutes were sexually inactive, virgins for life. Another reason to ridicule them! Although Christ, Mary, and oodles of Christian saints were revered for their virtuous abstinence, being a celibate Spinster was a shameful disgrace.

HOW THE SPINSTER GOT HER NAME

Spinning was one of the few jobs a woman could do for pay before she got married and took responsibility for a household and children. A woman who never married, either by will or circumstance, was doomed to spin for the rest of her life. Thus, she became a Spinster. It was an old custom to append the word to an unmarried woman's name. She would be known as Spinster Smith, Spinster Costello, Spinster Puddingsworth.

The card game Old Maid is played with a 33-card deck. All the cards are dealt out and players make as many pairs as they can from their hand. Then they draw cards from one another until all are paired, except the Old Maid, which has no match. The player left holding the Old Maid card is the loser and becomes the Old Maid.

Throughout history, wars have been very good at creating Spinsters. No men, no brides. By the end of the 19th century, there were 10 percent more women than men in Britain. The Civil War produced a similar ratio in the U.S. These unmarried women went off to work—in factories, primary schools, nursing, textiles and home design, advertising, and domestic service. They must have liked the freedom that came with earning a salary because soon one-quarter to one-third of all British women remained unmarried, many presumably by choice.

Education created Spinsters, too. The more women became educated, the less they got married! Between 1880 and 1900, 10 percent of all women in the U.S. were single, but a whopping 50 percent of those who went to college remained Spinsters their entire lives. Did they learn something new in school? Or was it just that, even then, men didn't like smart women?

By the end of the 19th century, women had won the right to keep their wages, own property, inherit wealth, and even to divorce. But it was still not okay for them to live alone. Some working women from the middle and upper classes banded together and lived as extended families. They formed what was known as "Boston marriages," complete with shared beds, love letters, and anniversary celebrations.

One celebrated Boston marriage was between four women known as the Red Rose Girls, after the Philadelphia estate where they lived. Three were prominent illustrators, the fourth acted as the housekeeper. They all took a secret surname, Cogs, an anagram of their initials, and pledged to live together forever. They were the toast of Philadelphia society for more than a decade until one partner was snatched away into a marriage opposed by the others. She was replaced with another woman and eventually the four split into two couples.

Whether or not Boston marriages were conjugal we will never know, but these liaisons were tolerated, even encouraged, by a Victorian society that believed women were sexual receivers who lacked libido. Were these couples just good friends, suffering through Spinsterhood together? The truth was, some probably were just friends. And many were a whole lot more.

The Red Rose Girls: Elizabeth Shippen Green, Violet Oakley, Jessie Willcox Smith, and Henrietta Cozens, Archives of American Art

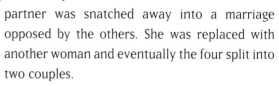

The late 19th century was filled with proud Spinsters who chose their unmarried state, and social scientists and psychologists who found new ways to denounce them. Groups like the Sexologists in Germany and the Motherhood Movement in the U.S. glorified maternity. To them, childless women were "surplus" and Spinsters were "the waste products of our female population." Some even proposed polygamy as a more suitable solution to the overpopulation of women.

Sexologists were progressive thinkers in one aspect: They observed that physical love between women was a fact. But they condemned Lesbians as "intermediate women," suited only for the most menial jobs where they could do minimal harm to society. This threatened the livelihoods of the many Lesbians in education and nursing, skilled women with broad access to children (see "Girls Who Do Girls," beginning on page 48).

As much as male society wished for women to stay barefoot and pregnant in the kitchen, an economic die was cast. In the 20th century (except for the postwar 1950s with its stay-at-home moms in the suburbs), women became essential to the workforce, meaning more women than ever were financially able to take care of themselves. And more and more women never married. At present, in the U.S. and Canada, there are two single women for every three who are wives.

It wasn't until 1965, when Helen Gurley Brown created *Cosmopolitan*, that a magazine encouraged single women to flaunt it. (*Flapper* magazine promoted modern lifestyles for women, so they could become modern wives.) Brown did more to fight the negative stereotype of the Old Maid/Spinster than almost anyone in publishing history. The Cosmo Girl was a swinging bachelorette: single, sexy, adventurous, and fun. In *Cosmo*, women could read lots of articles about how to find a man and get him to give her what she wanted in bed, but rarely an article about how to convince him to marry her. That's progress!

So what's with the current multibillion-dollar industry that tries to help unmarried women

> On opening night of Wendy Wasserstein's Pulitzer Prize-winning play, *The Sisters Rosensweig*, Wasserstein's mother said she was proud of her playwright daughter, "but wouldn't it have been nicer if this was Wendy's wedding?"

AND YOU THOUGHT SINGLE GUYS HAD MORE FUN? According to recent statistics, bachelors have more problems than bachelorettes: They don't live as long, they are in worse health, they commit more crimes, and they are more likely to be treated for alcoholism or drug abuse.

DY'S GIRL TOMBOY GIRL NEXT DOOR BIMBO FEMME FATALE/VAMP BITCH/BALLBREAKER GOOD/BAD MOTHER SPINSTER/OLD MAID HAG/CRONE

find husbands? Books and magazines on the subject abound, admonishing females to change their self-centered ways and make themselves more appealing to the opposite sex. A personality disorder called "The Old Maid Syndrome" is used to describe the growing number of single women over 30 who haven't found a satisfying relationship. Spinster Lit is the tag for a genre of pop fiction in the U.K. that tells of the perils and anxieties of young, unmarried women, also known as Singletons. These characters are all working girls, neurotically fixated on their single status. This brings us back to Bridget Jones and Ally McBeal. On the other hand, unmarried men are swinging bachelors, slightly suspect for their "commitment phobia," but envied for not being "tied down."

Today, a majority of women still get married, although the percentage is declining as more couples live together, are open about their homosexuality, or just choose to be alone. There are more single women than ever before, and a lot of them are happy about it! A group of Happily Unmarried Women call themselves Leather Spinsters and operate a Web site concerned with issues and information about being female and single. The Guerrilla Girls propose that the stereotype of the Spinster/Old Maid be one of the first exhibits in our soon-to-be-built Museum of Extinct Stereotypes.

Spinsters past and present, top to bottom: the Brontë sisters painted by their brother Patrick Branwell Brontë ca. 1834 (National Picture Gallery, London); Emily Dickinson; Greta Garbo (©Bettmann/Corbis); Condoleeza Rice (©Reuters NewMedia/Corbis)

They're not Spinsters in real life, just on TV: the *Sex and the City* girls have redefined being single. ©AFP/Corbis

Hag/Crone

Okay, you've survived Daddy's Girl, Tomboy, Girl Next Door, Bimbo, Bitch, Vamp, Motherhood, or Spinsterhood. What's next? The epithet Old Hag: an ugly, shriveled-up woman with straggly gray hair and missing teeth, hunched over a pot, brewing up trouble and misery for all. The stereotype of old women as repulsive and meddlesome starts with the Furies and Harpies of Greek mythology, runs through Shakespeare's witches in Macbeth to Madame Defarge and Miss Havisham in Dickens to the Wicked Witch of the West in the *Wizard of Oz.*

Few parallel stereotypes exist for aging men: Old Fart and Dirty Old Man come to mind, but they're more modern, and the Dirty Old Man has an enviable side: He gets credit for still having a sex drive.

Our culture turns aging women into evil shrews instead of venerating them as wise women as in Africa, China, South America, and among Native Americans. Because women in the West are devalued as they get older, many hide their age instead of celebrating it.

What happens to an older woman that diminishes her in society's view? For one thing, she experiences menopause and can no longer bear children. When birth control was rare and childbirth was more dangerous, life expectancy for women was considerably lower, and fewer women reached menopause. Now 22 percent of the population is women over 50, and you'd think things would be getting better for them! But some doctors continue to regard menopause as a disease or deficiency rather than as a natural process that happens to every woman after a certain age. More than a few gynecologists should be ashamed of the cruel treatments they've devised (see next page).

RHYMES WITH BITCH:

From the mid-16th to mid-18th centuries, over eight million women were executed as witches, many of them spinsters or widows without the protection of a husband. Some were also midwives and healers: older, independent women with special experience, intuitive powers, and a knowledge of herbal medicine that didn't fit "the program."

And then there's the fashion industry. Despite the fact that older women have more money to spend, the advertising world continues to serve up an endless supply of perfect young female bodies to make women of all ages feel inadequate! That's why we love the ladies of Rylestone, England, who bared their midlife

> Menopause must at last be recognized as a major medical problem in modern society... even the most valiant woman can no longer hide the fact that (after menopause) she is, in effect, no longer a woman.
> —Robert A. Wilson, M.D., *Forever Feminine*, best-selling book of 1968

(Wilson was a prime proponent of estrogen for menopausal women. In the summer of 2002, estrogen was discovered not to be the wonder drug previously believed. It also came out that Dr. Wilson's research and book were bankrolled by drug manufacturers.)

bodies in a nude calendar and made big bucks for charity.

The natural process of aging ushers in a new, unique phase in women's lives. Human females are the only members of the animal kingdom who can live half a lifetime after our reproductive years! Women "of a certain age" are no longer preoccupied with their roles as mothers and caregivers. Through widowhood or divorce, many are no longer defined by a relationship to a partner. They're free to take on all kinds of new challenges. Society may not celebrate our maturity and freedom, but we can.

SOME EARLY TREATMENTS FOR MENOPAUSE

LIVE BETTER WITH ELECTRICITY

In 1856, George Apostoli, a Frenchman obsessed with menopause and electricity, hooked up rods and wires to a primitive battery and delivered electric shocks directly into the uteruses of women suffering from a myriad of symptoms attributed to menopause. This ushered in an age of electro-gynecology. Funny how many of the women felt so cured by their first treatment, they didn't feel it necessary to sign up for a second! The practice was curtailed by 1920.

X-RATED TREATMENT

In 1905, Dr. Halberstadter found that rabbits ceased to ovulate when their ovaries were bombarded with X rays. Gynecologists rushed to use the same treatment on menopausal women suffering from heavy bleeding. The intent was to kill the ovaries and bring on menopause. The result was intestinal burns, ulcerated bowels, and dead patients.

The Guerrilla Girls present the following list of females, past and present, who defy stereotyped ideas of older women.

LATE BLOOMERS

Anna Mary Robertson "Grandma" Moses (1860-1961) grew up on a farm in rural New York. In her late 70s she picked up a paintbrush and started to record scenes from childhood memories. In a few short years she became one of the most beloved and best-known artists of the 20th century. Forget about what art historians think about her work, she was an antidote to the male stereotype that an important modern artist has to be a young, white guy who drinks too much.

Harriet Doerr (1910-2002) started college in 1927 and graduated in 1977. Her first novel, *Stones for Ibarra*, was published seven years later, when she was 73. It won the American Book Award.

Alma Thomas (1891-1978) was an artist who worked all her life as a school teacher, painting in her free time and during summer vacations. Only after retirement could she devote herself to it full time. She went on to a stellar career with shows at the Whitney Museum of American Art and the Corcoran Gallery of Art, all after the age of 80.

Golda Meir (1898-1978) began her political career at age 38, and became prime minister of Israel in 1969, at age 71. She held her own with big boys like Richard Nixon and Nikita Krushchev.

Mary Harris "Mother" Jones (1830-1930) left her life as a teacher and seamstress at 50 to become a labor organizer. She led the wives of striking miners in a famous broomstick standoff with strike breakers and marched to Washington to call attention to the injustices of child labor.

Lillian Gordy Carter (1898-1983), mother of President Jimmy Carter, was a registered nurse all her life. Instead of retiring, she joined the Peace Corps at 68 and spent several years in India.

Maggie Kuhn (1905-1995) took it personally when she was

WISE WOMEN IN OTHER CULTURES

Elder clan mothers among the Iroquois formed "sachems" that wielded real power within their matrilineal tribes: They nominated leaders and had approval power over lots of important tribal decisions like when to go to war and which treaties to sign.

Baianas are groups of respected elder women in the Samba lines at Carnival in Rio de Janeiro, who wear big hoop skirts and lead the parade.

forced to quit working at 65. She used her retirement years to form the Gray Panthers, an activist group that fought age discrimination and unfair pension practices.

AGELESS BABES

Here is a group of older women, as beautiful as any in a fashion magazine: Katharine Hepburn, Lena Horne, Judith Jamison, Sophia Loren, Yoko Ono, Chita Rivera, Gloria Steinem, Maria Tallchief, Tina Turner, Faye Wattleton.

WISE OLD WOMEN

If there were a Wise Old Woman stereotype in our culture, these women would qualify: Bella Abzug, Jane Addams, Marion Anderson, Susan B. Anthony, Helen Caldecott, Rachel Carson, the Delaney Sisters, Jane Goodall, Martha Graham, Fannie Lou Hamer, Dolores Huerta, Barbara Jordan, Queen Liliuokalani, Margaret Mead, Georgia O'Keeffe, Rosa Parks, Eleanor Roosevelt, Margaret Sanger, May Sarton, Annie Sullivan, Elizabeth Cady Stanton, Harriet Tubman, Sarah Winnemucca, Chien-Shiung Wu. We're sure you have your own wise women to add to this list.

Left to right: Maria Tallchief (©Bettmann/Corbis); Gloria Steinem (©Michael Brennan/Corbis); Rosa Parks (© AFP/Corbis); Eleanor Roosevelt; and Mother Jones (courtesy Library of Congress)

Chapter Three

THIS CHAPTER IS ABOUT SEX. OKAY, THE OTHER CHAPTERS ARE about sex , too, but this one is *really* about sex. Let's start with Girls Who Do but Not for Free: Harlot, Whore, Hussy, Call Girl, Hooker, Streetwalker, Lady of the Night, Woman of the Streets, Working Girl, Courtesan, Bawd, Cruiser, Strumpet, Procuress, Slut, Tart, Trollop, Floozy, Broad, Fly Girl, Tramp, Wench, Hoochie Mama, Ho, Hood Rat.

Sex objects:
Girls who do, girls who don't, girls who do girls

Girls Who Do but Not for Free

Why so many words in our language for prostitutes? Because the world's oldest profession has also been one of the largest. Social historians estimate that in the mid-19th century, one out of every ten women between the ages of 15 and 30 in New York City prostituted herself sometime during her life. Social reformers from the era calculated the number to be more like one in four. It's no wonder, since discrimination kept women out of just about every other kind of well-paying job.

Let's set the stage: It's 1843, and a young woman finds herself alone in New York or any other American city. She's an orphan or a widow. Maybe her husband left her with a handful of children. By law, she can't go to most schools, register for an apprenticeship, or

French ball in New York, *National Police Gazette,* late 19th century

Madam Sperber's brothel, Junction City, Kansas, 1906.
Joseph J. Pennell Collection, Kansas Collection,
University of Kansas Libraries

enter a trade. It's almost impossible for her to legally own property or run a business. She can't even get a divorce to marry another man who could support her.

What's the girl to do? Well, she could turn tricks on the street and earn enough to get by. Over time, she might find a steady job in a brothel or on a particular street corner. If she were clever, she might figure out a way to hire some other girls, set up a business, and become a Madam herself. Some of the most ambitious and successful businesswomen in history have been prostitutes.

Here's a statistic that made this particular career choice hard to pass up: In 1843, a woman sewing in a sweatshop earned 37 cents a day while a Streetwalker—the lowliest and lowest-paid kind of prostitute—could earn upward of $5 in a single night! Even by 1870, in the thick of the industrial revolution when a factory girl earned between $6 and $12 a week, a prostitute might earn $30 a night in saloons and $50 a week in the streets. Some of those factory girls were also hookers. Then, as now, most prostitutes turned tricks part time.

At the time, prostitution was looked upon as an inevitable by-product of human nature. Married men wanted more variety than they could get from their wives, so they went to prostitutes. Premarital sex was taboo, so unmarried men went, too. And there was the right of passage where a young male virgin was initiated into the mysteries of carnal knowledge by an older, wiser whore, paid for by the guy's friends or even his dad.

Abilene dance hall, from *The History of the Cattle Trade* by Joseph McCoy. Kansas State Historical Society, Topeka

Prostitute characters in literature before the 19th century were often lusty pleasure seekers like the bawds in Shakespeare, scheming courtesans in *Dangerous Liaisons*, and the charming Moll Flanders. All are in control of their lives and hardly exploited in their profession.

But the image of prostitutes over the last 150 years has not been so cheerful. We tend to think

HOW THE PIMP GOT HIS JOB:

In situations where prostitution is a dangerous job, working girls need protection. Many end up with pimps who manage them and just as often exploit them. But it wasn't always that way. During the golden age of brothels in the 19th century, each house had a security guard to keep things from getting rowdy. The first pimps were just that: beefy but lowly bodyguards in the employ of a Madam. When the brothel system went underground, pimps took the upperhand and moved into management.

of women who swap sex for money as sinful, pathetic, wretched victims of circumstance, and even as criminals.

How did the Happy Hooker of yore become the Fallen Woman? Let's go back to the middle of the 19th century when the brothel system, run pri-

IT'S ALMOST ALWAYS PROSTITUTES WHO GET ARRESTED AND JAILED, NOT THE MEN WHO HIRE THEM OR PIMP FOR THEM.

A Fallen Woman about to commit suicide, from *The Dangerous Classes of New York* by Charles Loring Brace, 1872

marily by women, collapsed and was replaced by a network of saloons, burlesque theaters, dance halls, and oddball museums where prostitutes could openly solicit clients if the cops and politicians were paid enough to look the other way. These new venues were run by, you guessed it, MEN, and income was drained away from the women who did the actual sex work. The modern sex industry, where prostitutes became exploited victims, was born.

In this corrupt atmosphere, the world's oldest profession became all tangled up in illicit, underground activities like drugs, smuggling, rum running, gambling, organized crime, white slavery, protection rackets, etc., all of which were secret, shady, and illegal but raked in a lot of money for the guys who controlled things. By association, sex work got a really bad rap and the law came down on prostitutes in a big way. It's almost always prostitutes who get arrested and jailed, not the men who hire, exploit, or abuse them,

AM PROSTITUTE WITH A HEART OF GOLD SLUT STREETWALKER STRUMPET TART TRAMP TROLLOP WENCH WHORE WORKING GIRL

even today. In New York state in 1993, 83 percent of the prostitution-related arrests were for soliciting. Only 11 percent of arrests were for patronizing a prostitute and only 6 percent were for pimping or promoting prostitution.

Nineteenth-century literature got into the act of condemning and degrading prostitutes, too. Fallen Women began to appear in pulp fiction, a genre that simultaneously titillated and moralized. Like Vamp movies of the 1920s and soap operas of today, this fiction played both sides of a culture war between Victorian repression and changing ideas about women's sexuality. It produced its own polar stereotypes: the Good Whore and the Bad Whore.

Destitute girls with no choice but to prostitute themselves to survive were looked upon with compassion and could become Good Whores. How? If they were transformed into Good Wives and Mothers when the right man showed up to save them. This stereo-type was and is rooted in the economic reality of many women.

But prostitutes who went into the profession for kicks or money and refused to give it up...oooooo, they were Bad Whores. They were given one-way tickets to hell.

While there are statistically fewer prostitutes now than in the 19th century, our culture is still obsessed with them. Moviemakers especially get off on these characters. So do their audiences. Just think of the famous actresses who have played working girls: Elizabeth Taylor in *Butterfield 8*, Catherine Deneuve in *Belle du Jour*, Jane Fonda in *Klute*, Julie Christie in *McCabe & Mrs. Miller*, Jodie Foster in *Taxi Driver*, Brooke Shields and Susan Sarandon in *Pretty Baby*, Julia Roberts in *Pretty Woman*, Elisabeth Shue in *Leaving Las Vegas*, Nicole Kidman in *Moulin Rouge*...the list goes on and on.

These Hollywood portrayals are not very nuanced, however. They usually just perpet-uate the retrograde Good Whore/Bad Whore straightjacket. The Good Whores get saved by rich, good-looking husbands, and the Bad Whores go crazy, drink too much, get sick, and die.

Whore stories are rarely written from the prostitute's point of view.

- BARBIE'S SORDID HISTORY
- As revealed by M.G. Lord in
- *Forever Barbie*, the world's
- best selling doll has some-
- thing in her past that she
- doesn't want you to know.
- Barbie started out as a
- teutonic cartoon hooker
- named Lilli who slept her
- way into the hearts of men
- all over Germany in the
- 1950s. She was then made
- into a jokey gift doll for
- men, complete with sexy,
- interchangeable clothes.
- Ruth Handler, owner of
- Mattel, discovered Lilli on a
- trip to Europe, bought the
- rights, cleaned her up a bit,
- renamed her, and the rest
- is history.

That's why, when a real-life hooker tells all, like Mayflower Madam Sydney Biddle Barrows, or Beverly Hills Madam Heidi Fleiss, they cause a sensation. The irony is that both these Girls Who Did are now making their living selling professional sex techniques to wives and girlfriends everywhere!

One of the biggest quandaries feminists find themselves in today is what to think about prostitutes and sex work. Does prostitution degrade and damage women or is it a service profession, a business, a job, like any other?

The Guerrilla Girls think there is a more important issue to be considered. In a culture where sex is everywhere and women are reduced to sex objects at every turn, when exactly does the sale of sex begin? All those naked female bodies on magazine covers plastered all over newsstands are selling sex. Are they prostitutes? All the young female musicians who grind away at mikes with their navels and cleavage on display are selling sex, too. Are they prostitutes? And what about phone-sex operators who can get guys off with nothing but the sound of their voices? Are they prostitutes? What about Gold Diggers and Trophy Wives who exchange sex with their husbands for a luxurious lifestyle? Are Mistresses and Kept Women all that different from Call Girls?

At what point does the use of sex to earn money become prostitution? When someone can answer that question, the Guerrilla Girls promise to come up with an official attitude and policy toward Working Girls.

• • • • • • • • • • • • •

Here are some more stereotypes for Girls Who Do but Not for Free:

MADAM: An entrepreneurial woman who probably started out as a prostitute and ended up employing other working girls in a brothel or an escort agency. There was a higher percentage of

The verbs "to whore" and "to prostitute" have come to mean selling out or going against one's own moral system. That alone tells us where society stands on prostitution.

Why is the decision by a woman to sleep with a man she has just met in a bar a private one, and the decision to sleep with the same man for $100 subject to criminal penalties?
—Anna Quindlen, *The New York Times*, 1994

I was naughty. I wasn't bad.
Bad is hurting people,
doing evil. Naughty is
not hurting anyone.
Naughty is being amusing.
—Sydney Biddle Barrows,
the Mayflower Madam

Madams in New York City, say, a hundred and fifty years ago than there are today, but the stereotypical characteristics of the Madam haven't changed at all: She's a smart business-woman, something of a psychologist and a PR specialist who knows how to deal with her girls, their johns, and the vice squad as well. Brothel prostitutes—who have a steady, pre-selected clientele and the protection of a fierce Madam—are among the highest class of sex worker. The Madam controls their lives, but gives them higher pay and better working conditions than they'd get from a pimp. Madams are also the most literate of all prostitutes. When they get caught, they usually become writers.

CALL GIRL: A 20th-century stereotype inadvertently created by Alexander Graham Bell. Since the invention of the telephone, some working girls don't have to walk the street or hang around in brothels anymore. The stereotype has them lounging around their gorgeous apartments eating bonbons, doing their nails, and playing with their Shih Tzus, waiting for the phone to ring. Actually, most call girls are also students, models, or actresses working part time.

PROSTITUTE WITH A HEART OF GOLD: A Good Whore. She's Irma la Douce: sweet, caring, and a good listener. She gives her johns real affection and attention, making them feel special, maybe even loved. Or so they think. In reality, she's probably devoted to a pimp, or a pimpy boyfriend, who takes all her money.

DOMINATRIX: A woman hired by a john to order him around and add the element of pain to sex. She arrives with all the accoutrements of torture: leather, chains, a whip, straps, and paddles, ready to make a guilty, submissive man suffer for his own pleasure, according to his script. Prostitutes take on the dominatrix identity as part of their jobs, turning it on and off at a customer's request. Then there's the world of dominatrix specialists, who do nothing but S&M.

Dominatrices prop up the cliché that the more powerful a man is out in the world, the more he likes to be dominated in bed. Or is it the reverse—that women, who rarely have much power in the world, often get off by wielding the whip?

Leaders of countries called me and asked for sex. You look at any picture of a politician with some girls around him and three of them will be mine.
—Heidi Fleiss,
the Beverly Hills Madam

Photo courtesy Heidi Fleiss

STREETWALKER: The prostitute who picks up guys on the street is the lowest-paid and lowest-class whore. Because she'll do it with practically anyone who walks by, she's the most likely to need a pimp to protect her (and probably abuse her) or to be drug addicted or HIV infected. Her appearance is an advertisement for her profession: short skirts, fishnet stockings, thigh-high boots, lots of makeup, exposed cleavage. The Streetwalker is the most common stereotype of a prostitute, even though she comprises only 10 to 15 percent of the profession.

HO, HOOCHIE MAMA, SLUT, ETC.: The latest wrinkle in pop culture's love-hate relationship with whores is how often words for "prostitute" get leveled at women who aren't. Ho, Slut, Broad, and Wench all started out meaning "prostitute," became generic insults used to demean and belittle a woman, and now are used affectionately by guys to refer to their girlfriends. In contemporary street culture, men are proud to be called pimps—it means they're powerful and enviable. The Guerrilla Girls think this ho and pimp thang has gone far enough.

Objects of Affection

Today, a sexy woman can be a good girl. Here are some Girls Who Do and are loved for it.

PINUP GIRL: This stereotype began with Betty Grable, the voluptuous Almost Girl Next Door whose leggy photo kept up the spirits—and we know what else—of GIs fighting overseas in World War II. Soon real-life Girls Back Home started taking pictures of themselves in similar sexy poses to send to their boyfriends on the front lines. Before this moment, only bad girls allowed themselves to be photographed so scantily clad. Hugh Hefner went on to make a fortune from this idea

BOMBSHELL: This one sprang fully formed from the Jean Harlow movie of the same name in which she plays a nice Girl Next Door who got discovered and was transformed overnight into a

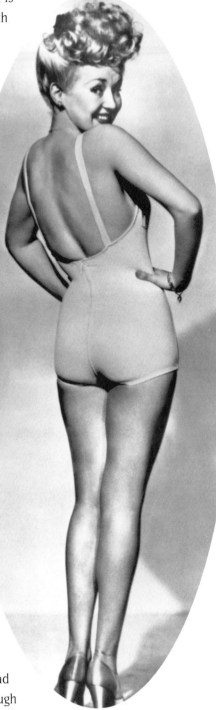

Betty Grable (© Bettmann/Corbis.)
This image was a big hit
during World War II.

Hollywood star. Everything the Bombshell did got attention; everyone she passed stopped dead in their tracks in her aura. Bombshells are not quite Dumb Blondes because they aren't dumb, even if some of them are blonde. Women don't mind being called Bombshells because it denotes power and influence, and drop-dead looks. Its usage in the press and media has never waned. But a male superstar would never be called a Bombshell as his power is not accidental or the result of someone finding him: It's inherent, inevitable, and deserved.

FOXY LADY: Black slang of the 1940s for a woman who was not only beautiful but also sexually attractive and provocative. The expression became big in the 1960s when Jimi Hendrix wrote a song of the same title. This is one sexual stereotype that is totally positive. There is hardly a woman alive who wouldn't want to be called a Foxy Lady. There are other sexual terms for women that compare them favorably to animals, like Sex Kitten, but even more are mean and nasty (see below).

Objects of Disaffection: The Animals Among Us

There are a whole slew of negative stereotypes to denigrate women by likening them to animals: Cow, Whale, Dog, Moose, Pig, etc. Usually these are comparisons based on a woman's appearance or size. Guerrilla Girls, who wear the masks of big, hairy, powerful jungle creatures whose beauty is hardly conventional, think these slurs are really animophobic. We believe all animals, large and small, like all women, large and small, are beautiful in their own way.

Girls Who Don't: Prude, Cocktease, Ice Queen, and Fag Hag

A girl who has sex may be called a Slut, a Nympho, and other nasty names—but sometimes it's even worse to be a girl who doesn't have sex. In our libido-driven society, the Girl Who Doesn't must have something wrong with her! There's the uptight Prude who won't let herself do it, the cruel Cocktease who leads a guy (or gal) on but won't deliver, the frigid Ice Queen who's alluring but can't be aroused, and the Fag Hag who can't handle sex at all and spends her life around gay men.

Girls Who Do and Do and Do

A Nymphomaniac, Nympho for short, is a girl with wild and uncontrollable sex urges. It's a stereotype derived from Greek mythology, where Nymphs were innocent young spirits who personified the elements of nature: wind, water, etc. They loved to sing, dance, and cavort with the gods. Until the 18th century, the word "nymph" was used to describe a young, beautiful, and gentle woman. Then it became the scientific name for a part of female genitalia, the labia minora. That was the end of its innocence. By the 19th century, a Nymphomaniac was a woman who had indiscriminate sex and was unable to form lasting relationships. Because women weren't supposed to enjoy sex and were expected to marry for life, this condition was declared a disease that necessitated medical attention and some pretty crude treatments, like clitorectomies.

Men love Nymphos because they put out, and they fear them because they are insatiable. Of course, they brag about their own promiscuity. How about basketball pro Wilt Chamberlain, who claimed he had sex with 20,000 women? It's only recently that men who've gotta have it over and over have been tagged with their own negative stereotype: Sex Addict. Some of these guys have held the top job in the U.S. government!

THE HIGH-SCHOOL SLUT

In her book, *Fast Girls: Teenage Tribes and the Myth of the Slut,* Emily White interviewed women who were known as sluts in high school. She found that many became sexually promiscuous only after being called a slut. They figured if they were stuck with the reputation anyway, what was the point of fighting it? Why were these girls unfairly tagged? Usually they had developed breasts early or were different in some other way—poor in an affluent school or recent immigrants.

Girls Who Do Girls

When we get to Girls Who Do Girls, at last we find a few female stereotypes invented by, for, and about women. Here is a list: Amy-John, Androdyke, Cofeminator, Dandysette, Dutch Girl, Dykeosaurus, Etelle, Fairy Lady, Gay Lady, Goose Girl, He-She, Lady-Lover, Lemonade, Les-Be-Friends, Lesbyterian, Mandyke, Muffet, Ruffle, Sistagirl, Tinkerbell, Tootsie, Two Spirit, and Zami.

The words "Lesbian" and "Sapphist" hearken back to the Greek poet Sappho in the seventh century B.C. Like other women of her class, which was upper, Sappho's official job was to marry, bear children, and pass on her family legacy. That might have kept her home a lot of the time, but it didn't keep her from developing a unique form of poetry and gathering a group of female devotees around her. She returned their admiration by writing bridal odes and love poetry for them, like this:

> I see he who sits near you as an equal of the gods
> For he can closely listen to your delightful voice
> And that seductive laugh
> That makes the heart behind my breasts to tremble.

Whether or not Sappho ever consummated her passion with these women doesn't really matter. That she came to represent the transgressive idea that a woman can desire another woman does. Throughout Western history, romantic love between women has been tagged "Sapphist." But in the late 19th century, when a term

Left to right, some Girls Who Did Girls: Sappho of Lesbos; Lady Troubridge painted by lover Romaine Brooks (Smithsonian American Art Museum/Art Resource, NY); Susan B. Anthony and Emily Gross, suffragists and life partners, circa 1896 (Sophia Smith Collection, Smith College); Rebecca Perot, 19th century Shaker leader (Western Reserve Historical Society); Edna St. Vincent Millay, poet (Arnold Genthe); Zora Neale Hurston, writer (Carl Van Vechten); Akiko Yosano, poet; Barbara Jordan, Congresswoman (Larry Murphy); Antonia Pantoja, Puerto Rican activist.

was finally needed to describe the growing phenomenon of many women loving women, it was the women around Sappho on her home island of Lesbos, not Sappho herself, who became their namesake. Lesbian consciousness and the Lesbian community were born. In the history of gay life, that was a very important moment.

Once the Love That Dare Not Speak Its Name finally got one, life as a Lesbian became even more complicated. While it had been perfectly respectable for upper- and middle-class spinster women to live together in "romantic friendships" in the late 19th century, come the 20th century, these partnerships were suspect. Social scientists and doctors realized women DO have sexual desires of their own and are not simply passive receptacles for male sexuality. It became obvious that these girls just might have something going on between the sheets!

Lesbianism became a category of sexual behavior, and the same "scientists" who identified it declared it as unnatural, a crime against nature, an inversion, a social vice, a disease. For decades psychologists, psychiatrists, social workers, and doctors tried to "cure" Lesbians and gay men of their homosexuality. It wasn't until 1973 that homosexuality was declassified as a mental disorder by the American Psychological Association.

The history of Girls Who Do Girls in the last century was a story of wide swings of liberation and tolerance followed by cruel repression: two steps forward, one step back.

Here's the pattern: At the turn of the 20th century, women started going to college in larger numbers. Many became self-supporting and never married. Some of these single women chose

Avoid girls who are too affectionate and demonstrative in their manner... When sleeping in the same bed with another girl, old or young, avoid "snuggling up" close together... and, after going to bed, if you are sleeping alone or with others, just bear in mind that beds are sleeping places. When you go to bed, go to sleep just as quickly as you can.
—Irving D. Steinhardt, *Ten Sex Talks With Girls 14 Years and Older*, 1914

to live as same-sex couples. They formed a discreet population of Lesbian professionals in education, nursing, and other fields open to women at the time. The Roaring Twenties and the Harlem Renaissance encouraged sexual and creative freedom, and Lesbian artists, writers, and musicians were an essential part of it all. They were mostly underground, but out among themselves.

The Great Depression of 1929 ushered in a conservative backlash against new female lifestyles. Loose, free Flapper clothes were replaced by girdles and uplift bras. Social scientists and medical doctors argued over whether homosexuality was congenital or environmental, but they agreed on one thing: All homosexuals were social deviants. Raids, arrests, jail, and even mental hospitals were the norm for any who were open about it. Gays first organized as a political force against their repression during the Weimar Republic in Germany (see sidebar, left). In the 1940s homosexuals became victims of the Nazi Holocaust, along with Jews and the insane.

But World War II had an interesting effect on Lesbian consciousness. With all the men away at war, there were millions of women left to find intimate solace with one another. Some lived as Lesbians while the boys were away. Other Lesbians joined the army to help in the war effort. There they became a community and lived and worked together without reprisal...as long as they kept it to themselves (see below).

After the war, homosexuals, male and female, were persecuted as never before by Senator Joseph McCarthy and the U.S. government. They were considered as great a risk to the postwar American way of life as communists. Gay bars and parties were raided regu-

Johnnie Phelps, from *Odd Girls and Twilight Lovers* by Lillian Faderman

HE ASKED, SHE TOLD

During World War II, General Dwight D. Eisenhower asked Sergeant Johnnie Phelps to root out the Lesbians in her company of the Women's Army Corps. Her answer: "Yessir...If the General pleases, I will be happy to do this investigation...But, sir, it would be unfair of me not to tell you, my name is going to head the list...You should also be aware that you're going to have to replace all the file clerks, the section heads, most of the commanders, and all the motor pool..." His response: "Forget the order."

larly, and Lesbians were harassed and lived in fear of losing their jobs, their homes, and their children.

But then, whew, things got better again. The sexual revolution of the 1960s and the Stonewall Riots of 1968 empowered Girls Who Do Girls to stand up, proclaim their identity, tell their secret stories, write their hidden histories, and be proud.

It's kind of fitting now to see the tables reversed: It's homophobia, not homosexuality, that's considered a sickness and a social disease! Once members of a secret lifestyle, closed to all but insiders, Lesbians today come in every age, color, walk of life, and attitude, and are free enough to alter existing stereotypes and create their own new ones.

Even Butches and Femmes are evolving. This polarity, long at the core of Lesbian culture, is being challenged today, especially by Lesbian feminists, as being based too much on a heterosexual model of masculine/feminine behavior.

BUTCH: A Lesbian who is a "culturally defined masculine female." This can mean anything from wearing male clothing to talking and acting like a guy to being interested in male-identified jobs and sports. Some are drawn to fighting and carrying guns. Butches may or may not be sexually aggressive. There are many shades of Butch from Soft Butch to Butchy Woman to the most masculine Butch of all, the Stone Butch. Stone Butches sometimes pass for men and often think of themselves as a gender all their own. A synonym is a Diesel Dyke. Some decide to have operations and change their biological sex. Some don't.

There are lots of stories of cross-dressing saints throughout history who might have qualified as Butch, the most famous being Joan of Arc. But social historians argue that it wasn't until the late 19th century that the term "Butch" was born. Women in Boston marriages (see page 32) weren't Butch: They dressed the part of proper society ladies and lived among the heterosexual world with little prejudice. (Painter Rosa Bonheur was an exception. She liked to dress as a man to paint but had

Gladys Bentley

BLACK AND BLUE AND GAY

In the 1920s and '30s, an active Lesbian community of Blues singers flourished in Harlem. Some were discreet, like Alberta Hunter and Bessie Smith, while others were flamboyantly out, like Ethel Waters, Ma Rainey, and Gladys Bentley (above)—who performed in a white tuxedo. Here are some lyrics from Ma Rainey:

PROVE IT ON ME BLUES
Went out last night, had a great
    big fight,
Everything seemed to go wrong;
I looked up, to my surprise,
The gal I was with was gone.

Where she went, I don't know,
I mean to follow everywhere
    she goes;
Folks say I'm crooked, I don't know
    where she took it,
I want the whole world to know:

They say I do it; ain't nobody
    caught me,
Sure got to prove it on me.
Went out last night with a
    crowd of friends,
They must have been women
    'cause I don't like no men.

Wear my clothes just like a fan,
Talk to the gals like any old man;
'Cause they say I do it, ain't nobody
    caught me,
Sure got to prove it on me.

GIRLZ2MEN

In eras when women had few rights, to dress as a man and to be thought of as male was to have privilege. It meant freedom to get a job, to own property, to move about unaccosted, to love a woman, to be a father. If discovered or caught, it could mean disgrace, disenfranchisement, even jail. History is filled with tales of women who dressed as men, some for their entire lives, from Joan of Arc to the hundreds of women who fought as male soldiers in the Civil War. Their reasons were as varied as their backgrounds. Many might never have considered themselves Lesbians. Some were clearly not. Here are a few good stories:

When **Dr. James Barry** died in 1865, he was discovered to have been the first FEMALE physician in Great Britain. Historians suspect that a group of aristocrats in support of education for women helped the daughter of an Irish grocer get a place in an all-male medical school in Edinburgh. For that, she became James Barry and went on to be a highly respected doctor who traveled the world and transformed the practice of medicine and surgery. Dr Barry performed one of the earliest successful Caesarean sections. He was popular and well liked by women. How popular, we'll never know.

Mary Fields (1832-1914) kept her name and even wore a skirt over her trousers and boots, but everything else about her life on the frontier was macho. A patchwork of jobs took her from slavery in Tennessee to cowboy country. At one point she drove a stagecoach and was known as Stagecoach Mary. Formidable at 200 pounds, she wore a revolver strapped to her waist and was the only woman allowed to drink in the saloons of Cascade, Montana. Known as a brawler who used her gun to settle scores, Mary was also loved by her neighbors and their children, who took a school holiday on her birthday.

Luisa Capetillo's cross-dressing was immortalized by a folk song in her native Puerto Rico and led to an arrest during a trip to Cuba. Capetillo (1879-1922) was a socialist, union organizer, author, feminist, and single mother of three.

Ralph Kerwinieo started life as Cora Anderson. A Native American, Ralph witnessed discrimination and genocide firsthand. He chose to pass as a man but he was a kind of feminist, too. He claimed he married one of his two wives to protect her from a sexist world. Here is a statement he made circa 1914: "The world is made for man...In the future centuries it is probable that woman will be the owner of her own body and the custodian of her own soul. But until that time you can expect the statutes [concerning] women will be all wrong. The well-cared-for woman is a parasite, and the woman who must work is a slave...Do you blame me for wanting to be a man?...Do you blame me for hating to again resume wearing a woman's clothes?"

Billy Tipton (1914-1989) was born Dorothy Tipton in Oklahoma City. At 19 she transformed herself into Billy Lee to get a job as a sax player in a jazz band. Billy stayed in drag the rest of his life, marrying five times, playing music, and later becoming a booking agent. When he died at age 74, his secret came out and was coast-to-coast news. It's not clear if all his wives knew the truth. To his adopted children, Bill was "just Dad."

Left to right: Barry; Fields (Naiad Press); Capetillo (Yamila Azize-Vargas collection); Kerwinieo (Jonathon Ned Katz collection); Tipton (AP/World Wide Photos)

Gay pride parade
© Joseph Sohm, ChromoSohm/Corbis

to get a police permit to do it. She wore dresses for social occasions and in photographs but wore male garb around the house.)

But working-class women who wanted to live in same-sex partnerships had to work to support themselves. To earn a living wage, this meant working jobs usually held by men. To do that, many ran away from their homes and backgrounds and disguised themselves as men. Some fought in wars as soldiers. Some spent their entire lives as men. (See "Girlz2Men," left.) Historians believe the masculinized behavior and dress of the modern Butch evolved from these individuals.

BULL DYKE (BD): First started as Boondagger or Bull Dagger, African-American slang for a tough, aggressive black Lesbian. Featured prominently in the lyrics of blues songs from the 1920s, like the "B.D. Woman's Blues," sung by Bessie Jackson.

FEMME: A Lesbian whose appearance and behavior approximates the cultural norm for feminine but who prefers same-sex partners, often a Butch. Shades of this stereotype include Lipstick Lesbians, and High Femmes who wear makeup, dresses, and high heels.

LESBIAN CHIC
In the late 1990s the media discovered Lesbians and declared them cool.

IT SEEMS TO BE THE SEASON FOR LESBIAN CHIC

Lesbian chic both blessing and curse

Pretty women and lesbian chic

Why is it in for lesbians to be out? The new wave of lesbian chic looks suspiciously like old-style male sexual fantasy.

Publishing, film and clothing put stamp of approval on lesbian chic

OH, THE LESBIAN CHIC OF IT ALL...

FLUFF: An ultrafeminine Femme.

BLUFF: Someone who plays both Butch and Femme roles.

KIKI: Lesbian who is neither Butch nor Femme: Looked on with suspicion by pure Butches and Femmes.

TOP: Dominant sexual partner.

BOTTOM: Passive sexual partner.

GRANOLA, CRUNCHY, HAIRY LESBIAN: A vegan, environmentalist Lesbian.

Girls Who Do Girls and Boys

Okay, we admit it, we haven't found many stereotypes for bisexuals. In fact, about the only one we could think of is LUG, (Lesbian Until Graduation). That's the college girl who experiments with women while in school, then goes hetero when she gets her diploma. Maybe there are so few stereotypes for bisexuals because there are still so many arguments over whether bisexuality is a legit sexual orientation or just fence-sitting. The Guerrilla Girls' opinion on the dispute: Human sexuality is fluid and ever changing. History is filled with great hetero, homo, and bi women whose lives and lifestyles all need to be acknowledged.

Chapter Four

MANY REAL WOMEN LED LIVES THAT BECAME STEREOTYPES. SOME earned this status because they were so good (Florence Nightingale, Mother Teresa), others because they were so evil (Tokyo Rose). Groups of real women (Flapper, Bra Burner) became stereotypes, too. There are stereotypes created by novelists (Lolita) and even corporations (Aunt Jemima, Betty Crocker). Here are our stereotyped life lessons, in chronological order.

Life lessons:
Real and fictional women who became stereotypes

Florence Nightingale

The stereotype: A woman who selflessly devotes her life to nursing the sick. The person: She was born in 1820 into an upper-class British family. Her father made the mistake of educating her, then expecting her to want no more from life than marriage to a wealthy man. Instead, she rejected a longtime suitor at the age of 30, became a confirmed Spinster, and developed a messianic zeal to improve public health. Hospitals then were dingy, unsanitary holes where only soldiers or the poor were treated. Nurses were usually prostitutes, alcoholics, and criminals. No surprise that her family objected. So, she picked up and went to study country nursing in Germany. Seven years later she returned to England and was appointed superintendent of a women's hospital in London. She quickly became an international hero for her unrelenting campaign to establish nursing as a respected profession, based on principles of sanitation and modern medicine.

When war broke out in 1854 in Crimea, Florence volunteered as a lowly field nurse but was soon running the whole nursing operation. Some of the things she did were simple: ordering 200 brushes to scrub down the filthy hospital, and washing the patients' clothes and bedsheets. Everywhere she went she rankled the all-male administrations and also some of the nurses of the old school who still sold favors on their evening rounds. But her public image as a near-saint helped her defy the powers that were. (Her family contacts didn't hurt, either.) Fatalities in her hospital dropped dramatically. She learned to deal with all sorts of powerful men and even had to spurn lots of new suitors.

Back in England after the war, Florence took to her bed with an unexplained illness, perhaps a bacterial infection she picked up in Turkey. She spent the remaining 50 years of her life as a semi-invalid. From her bed, she established the first school of nursing in Great Britain and wrote a number of important books on nursing and public health that are still in use today.

Aunt Jemima,
circa 1920 to
today.

Poor Aunt Jemima
Had to Mix
Everything
Herself!

Now—her famous recipe comes ready m

Tempt Yo' Appetite
MORNIN'
NOON or
NIGHT
AUNT JEMIMA PANCAKES

Aunt Jemima

Mention her name to white Americans and the aroma of fresh pancakes fills their senses, along with the image of a kindly, jovial black woman who wants nothing but to serve and dote on them. To African-Americans, another image comes to mind: an uneducated, servile black woman who doesn't realize slavery is over. She's an offensive racial stereotype fabricated by white businessmen to sell their product. One of the longest-lived icons in American advertising, Aunt Jemima is also one of the most controversial. Who is she and why, after all these years, can we still find her hanging out on grocery shelves trying to make us buy her pancake mix?

Aunt Jemima never was a real person. She was created by entrepreneurs Chris Rutt and Charles Underwood in the 1890s. They used the stereotype of the Southern black Mammy and a nostalgia for the antebellum South to sell their new invention: instant pancake mix. The false familiarity of the salutation "Aunt" mimicked the way black domestic slaves had been belittled in the South. Rutt and Underwood based her character on a minstrel show act, and on a popular song. They even hired a real person, Nancy Green, an African-American born in slavery in 1834, to flip thousands of pancakes at the Chicago World's Fair in 1894. She was a sensation and signed a lifelong contract to be the "spokes-mammy" for Aunt Jemima.

After Ms. Green's death in 1923, at least six other women were hired to appear as Aunt Jemima in public, giving demonstrations at state fairs, conventions, and on radio and TV. Quaker Oats, which owns the Aunt Jemima brand, went so far as to invent myths and legends to make people believe there really was an Aunt Jemima, even though at times three Aunt

A CROCK OF BETTY

In 1921, a company that eventually became General Mills received so many letters from women with baking questions, it cooked up Betty Crocker to respond to them. Her official signature was selected from women employees' handwriting samples. The last name of a retiring exec was combined with a first name judged to be reassuring and homey. It worked! Women really believed there was a professional out there who could help them solve their cooking and homemaking problems. In 1945, Betty Crocker was the second most admired women in America after Eleanor Roosevelt!

Betty wrote over 200 cookbooks, starred in hundreds of radio programs and even taught Gracie Allen how to cook on TV! Naturally (or is it unnaturally?) all Betty's meal ideas include General Foods products, like Hamburger Helper, instant potatoes, fake bacon, articially flavored cakes, aerosol frostings, and microwave popcorn.

Eighty years later, Betty is still at work and—miracle of miracles—actually getting younger! Her first image, created in 1936, shows her aging, gray, and stern-faced. At last sighting her skin had become olive-toned and her hair darkened in a gesture toward ethnic diversity. She's now a computer composite of a number of American female types. That's our Betty!

Above, Betty Crocker in 1936, and today.

Jemimas were on the road at once. She was given a husband, Uncle Mose, and two children. The most preposterous chapter in her invented life story was the time "When Robert E. Lee Stopped at Aunt Jemima's Cabin" and the legendary mammy happily cooked up stacks of delicious pancakes to fortify the Confederate officers who were leading an army to keep her enslaved.

Aunt Jemima endured as a brand name, despite protests and boycotts by African-Americans starting as early as 1916. Quaker Oats ignored early marketing studies in the 1930s that showed how offensive black Americans found her. And the company continued to find talented actresses and models willing to portray her for the right price, especially since there were few other roles available. (The first African-American woman to win an Oscar for Best Supporting Actress was Hattie McDaniel for her portrayal of the mammy in *Gone with the Wind*.)

When Disneyland opened in 1955, one of the restaurants in Frontier Town was called Aunt Jemima's. At least in this incarnation Aunt Jemima had finally become a business owner. The restaurant was closed a few years after the Yippies stormed the theme park in 1970, threatening to smoke pot with Tom Sawyer, liberate Tinkerbell, and hold a breakfast meeting with the Black Panthers at Aunt Jemima's Pancake House.

By the mid 1960s it had become a common insult to call another African-American a "raghead" or "handkerchief head." Aunt Jemima was right up there next to Uncle Tom as an epithet for a black sellout to white values. In spite of all the protests, Quaker Oats refused give up Aunt Jemima. Instead, the company slowly changed her. In 1968, the same year Martin Luther King Jr. was assassinated, her handkerchief was transformed into a headband. Overnight, she became thinner and younger.

In 1989, the headband came off, her hair was streaked with gray, and she began to wear earrings, implying that maybe she was now a working mother with some money to spend on herself. Quaker Oats even hired another working mother, singer Gladys Knight, to be a spokesperson for the product. Three hundred million dollars in annual sales was far more important to Quaker Oats than discontinuing a divi-

- Not a real Aunt
- Jemina box, but
- it was perfect in
- the Black Power
- 1960s.

No More, 1967. Painting by Jon Onye Lockard

sive symbol of our racist history. That's why we still find Aunt Jemima in stores next to Uncle Ben with his rice and Rastus hawking Cream of Wheat.

In March of 2002, the Aunt Jemima Brand of Quaker Oats donated $100,000 to the National Council of Negro Women. Guerrilla Girls think that's small potatoes in reparations for nearly a century of keeping Aunt Jemima, as writer M. M. Manning has observed, a "slave in a box."

Flapper

After the 19th amendment gave women the right to vote, all hell broke loose. A mass of young women, calling themselves Flappers, invented a new modern lifestyle and jettisoned many of the conventions of female behavior that society held sacrosanct. Wild women like Zelda Fitzgerald, Isadora Duncan, Josephine Baker, and Louise Brooks were considered Flappers. It was the first youth movement of the 20th century, and it was exclusively female.

The name Flapper probably came from the fledgling young bird who makes a commotion learning to fly out of its nest. Between 1920 and the Great Depression of 1929, Flappers caught on like wildfire. They had their own magazine, their own national organizations called "flocks," their own slang. They wrote manifestos, held beauty contests and garnered supporters and detractors, the latter affectionately called "slappers." As *Flapper* mag-

$100 for a Flapper

THE FLAPPER
Not for Old Fogies
JUNE
20 Cents A Copy
25c In Can.
TRADE MARK
Two Dollars A Year
$2.50 In Can.

Flapper Styles Will Prevail!

THE FLAPPER
Not for Old Fogies
OCTOBER
20 CENTS A COPY
[TRADE MARK]
TWO DOLLARS A YEAR

P and A PHOTO

N—ASK MYRNA

PER? Impossible!

"THE FLAPPER'S REVENGE" in This Number

- Before Flappers
- there were Gibson
- Girls, (pictured right)
- a mass fashion fad
- inspired by the looks
- and style of Irene
- Gibson and immor-
- talized by her artist
- husband Charles
- Dana Gibson.
- Gibson Girls were
- considered the epit-
- ome of femininity
- from 1895 until the
- Flapper era of the
- 1920s. Their clothing
- was constricting,
- their demeanor
- demure, but they
- did dare to do a
- few modern things,
- like riding bicycles
- and playing golf,
- both newfangled
- inventions.

azine put it in 1922: "A revolution has occurred of greater significance than the French revolution, the Russian revolution or even perhaps our own revolution of 1776. The Flappers have rebelled—and by that act of rebellion they have not only justified their existence, but insured their survival."

A Flapper wore her beliefs on her body and could be spotted a block away. She cut off her long hair and invented the bob, the shingle, and other short, streamlined hairstyles for women. She threw off the long, heavy dresses of the previous era and donned lighter, more comfortable, functional clothes. Out went the bustles, corsets, and whalebone stays laced so tight they made her mother faint. In came scandalous one-piece step-in lingerie that revealed the real shape of her body beneath. If that wasn't shocking enough, Flappers wore makeup, previously reserved for prostitutes. They exercised for their health wearing sports clothes like knickers that actually allowed them to move! They swam in one-piece bathing suits and often got arrested for it. They rolled their stockings down to the knee so the tops showed. In summer they went out with bare, tanned legs. Even more shocking!

What's more, Flappers went out with whomever they chose, no longer asking parental permission or taking along a chaperone. This libertine behavior ushered in the modern date. They smoked and drank in public, something only men did before. They danced the Charleston, the shimmy and the black bottom with abandon, made out at "petting parties"

BEFORE FLAPPERS

and in the backseats of cars. Worst of all, some of them even engaged in pre-marital sex or same-sex sex! Some left home and never came back!

Soon the Flapper image became a fashion statement for all sorts of women in the 1920s who wanted to be modern: young, old, and in between. Everyone's grandmother, great-grandmother, or great-great-grandmother who lived through this period can tell a story about the first woman in her family to bob her hair or smoke a cigarette.

We 21st-century girls have a lot to thank the Flappers for. They left us plenty of slang we still use today: lounge lizard (ladies' man); jazz baby (a Flapper); bozo (dull guy); ducky (good); cough up (pay up); baloney (ridiculous); keen, nifty (good); mixer (people getting together); all dolled up (dressed up); peppy (energetic); and dud (a shy person). They also invented slang terms that we don't use today but are pretty funny: cheaters (glasses); button shining (close dancing); drop the pilot (get a divorce); prune pit (anything old-fashioned); boob tickler (a girl who entertains her father's out-of-town customers); and fig leaf (bathing suit).

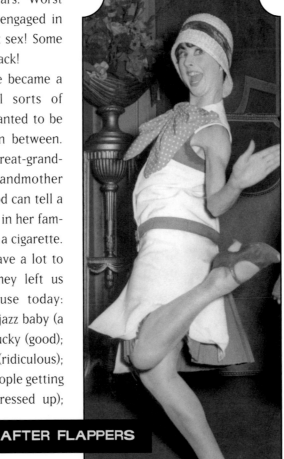
© Bettmann/Corbis

AFTER FLAPPERS

Flappers represented a new, collective spirit of free women who wouldn't take no for an answer, who weren't going to sit back and accept only what was given to them. They had won their rights, they were going to exercise them, AND they were going to have a good time doing it!

The events of the Depression and the Second World War ended the Flapper era. But women were on their way.

Carmen Miranda

Which came first...the woman or the stereotype? Carmen Miranda (1909-55) spent her first 5 years in her native Portugal and her last 15 in the U.S. But to the world she was always Brazil. She popularized street songs and sambas and gave Brazilian music a new face. Her signature costume, later exaggerated even more in Hollywood, was based on the traditional dress of black Baianas in northern Brazil, who carried fruit and vegetables to market on their heads. By 1939, Carmen was a beloved icon throughout South America. Once lured to the U.S., American-style success was too much to resist. She returned to Brazil only twice before her death.

In the early 1940s, the Hollywood entertainment machine extruded extravagant musicals with South American themes. Nelson Rockefeller, coordinator of Inter-American Affairs for the U.S. government, and John Hay Whitney, head of the CIA film division, encouraged these concoctions, believing they would create goodwill between North and South America at a time when much of the world was at war. South America was presented as white, cheerful, and without social unrest.

In these films Carmen became a cliché of exotic Pan-Latin-ness that could only have succeeded in Anglo culture. Everything about her was exaggerated. Her turbans reached legendary heights. So did her open-toed platform shoes. Her peasant skirts were studded with sequins and glitter. Always in high gear, she played the Latin spitfire to the hilt. By 1945, Carmen Miranda was the highest-paid woman in show business.

Americans loved her films, but South Americans felt they were superficial and

- BANANAS WAS HER
- BUSINESS?
- Then Carmen
- Miranda must have
- been a Guerrilla Girl.

BEST DOCUMENTARY

Carmen MIRANDA

Bananas is my Business

Poster from Helena Solberg's 1994 documentary

offensive. *Down Argentine Way* was banned in Argentina. Brazilians were annoyed that Carmen portrayed herself as the embodiment of their country, but her music mixed Brazilian samba with Caribbean rumba. Some believed it was a disgrace that she preferred to be a financially successful one-dimensional stereotype in the U.S. rather than a flesh-and-blood artist back home.

Although her public persona was relentlessly upbeat, the life of the Latin Bombshell did not have a happy ending. In her last roles Carmen Miranda played a parody of herself, mouthing lines that made fun of what she had become. Scripts continued to be written in her early fractured English when she no longer spoke that way.

Driven by her work schedule and ignoring her own health, Carmen Miranda collapsed in the middle of an appearance on the Jimmy Durante show in 1955 and died the next day. In death she became a Carioca again. Her funeral in Rio was attended by thousands, and her grave is a must-see for her ever-growing legion of fans. Her iconic style is kept alive by scores of drag queens who adopt her fruit-adorned costumes for Carnival.

It's interesting to speculate on what might have happened to Carmen Miranda if she had stayed in Brazil. Her talent and ambition were unquestionable. She was star material from the get-go. What kind of an artist might she have become if she were not the exotic "other" but the best among many?

CARMEN MIRANDA'S SONG ABOUT HERSELF AS A STEREOTYPE:

I loff to wear my hair like Deanna Durbin but I have to stoof eet een a turban... A turban that weighs 5,433 pounds. And not only that, but I have to wear those crazy gowns!

I make $10,000 a week, but does that make me happee? Of course eet does. But eef I queet my job eet's not disturbin'... I'm better off than Ingrid Bourbon 'cause I can seet at home and eat my turban!

Left: Carmen Miranda paper doll
© Tom Tierney, 1982.
Above: Miranda © Bettmann/Corbis

63

Mother Teresa on the path to sainthood, on the cover of *Catholic Digest*, February 1999

Mother Teresa

Mother Teresa, born Agnes Gonxha Bojaxhiu in Yugoslavia in 1910, believed from the age of 12 that she had a mission to serve the poor. She joined an order of Irish nuns and went to Calcutta at age 18. First she was a schoolteacher, then she set up a school and clinic for homeless children. By the time Mother Teresa died in 1997, hundreds of doctors and nurses and social workers staffed her clinics all over the world. She had inspired countless others to devote themselves to good works, too. She had won the Nobel Prize and the U.S. Presidential Medal of Freedom. She was a living, breathing saint. Now that she's dead, the campaign is already under way to canonize her as a real saint. Her name became synonymous with selflessness.

That was the stereotype. Behind the scenes, Mother Teresa was more interested in treatment than in prevention. She railed against the crushing poverty that affects so many of the world's children, but opposed birth control. In her Nobel acceptance speech, she called abortion and birth control the single greatest threats to world peace. Hmmmm. "There can no more be too many babies than there can be too many flowers or stars," was her creed.

Never too many awards or donations either. Mother Teresa accepted them no matter what the source. When Papa Doc Duvalier, the strongman of Haiti, gave her an award, she praised his love for the poor, instead of condemning his corrupt regime for creating poverty in Haiti.

She accepted $1.4 million from Charles Keating, who embezzled hundreds of millions from bank depositors in the United States. A court asked her to give it back. She never did. We bet that some of the people whose life savings Keating destroyed were the kind who, had they lived in India and suffered a severe financial setback, just might have to abandon a baby.

One last social problem she was an expert on: love and marriage. When the Republic of Ireland, thousands of miles from her home in India, held a referendum on divorce in 1995, Mother Teresa urged voters to ban it. Her orthodoxy didn't keep her, however, from expressing relief at the divorce of her good friend, Princess Diana.

Tokyo Rose

A Tokyo Rose is an evil female traitor who uses her sexuality to beguile and betray. The stereotype grew out of the tragic story of Iva Ikuko Toguri d'Aquino, an American born on the Fourth of July, 1916.

The dutiful daughter of Japanese immigrants, Iva graduated from UCLA, then left for Japan as her family's representative at a relative's sickbed. That was 1941. When the war broke out, Iva was trapped in a country whose language she didn't speak and where, as a U.S. citizen, she was an alien enemy overnight. Her relatives didn't even want anything to do with her! She found a job as an English-language typist for Radio Tokyo. There she caught the attention of an Australian prisoner of war, Charles Cousens, who had been ordered to write Japanese propaganda. He thought Iva's voice was strident and sexy and perfect for a new radio show.

So started the "Zero Hour," a weekly radio program broadcast throughout the South Pacific on Sunday evenings. Iva and more than a dozen other English-speaking women appeared on it, each with a pseudonym. Hers was Orphan Ann—an apt description of her situation. None were named Tokyo Rose. That was a media invention that came later.

Orphan Ann would come on the air with a message like this: "Greetings, everybody. This is your number-one enemy, your favorite playmate Orphan Ann from Radio Tokyo. The little sunbeam whose throat you'd like to cut. All you poor, abandoned soldiers, sailors, and marines vacationing on those lovely tropical islands. Gets a little hot now and then, doesn't it? Well, just remember, fellas, while you're sweating it out on the islands, your sweet little patootie back home is having a hotcha time with some friendly defense worker. They're probably dancing right now to this number...it used to be your song...remember?" Then they'd play some Benny Goodman or Glenn Miller song.

This was supposed to demoralize the GIs. But Allied commanders thought the messages actually built up morale and helped instill a fighting spirit, sort of like those drill sergeants who use

Top: Tokyo Rose broadcasting.
Bottom: Tokyo Rose goes to jail,
photo: National Archives

insults to motivate. The generals gave Iva a citation after the war, especially because she refused to denounce her U.S. citizenship.

But the U.S. government took a different view. They imprisoned her for 12 months in Japan. In 1948, when she wanted to return to the States, there was a public outcry to lynch her, led by Walter Winchell, the American Legion, the Native Sons and Daughters of the Golden West, and the Los Angeles City Council, whose members officially opposed her return. They feared she might incite other Japanese Americans who had just been released from internment camps (Iva's parents among them). Her husband was not allowed in the country; she miscarried their child. The press flung the label "Tokyo Rose" at her. And it stuck.

Although there was little real evidence, she was put on trial. It became a media event and cost half a million dollars in 1948. The judge refused the jury's request for a dismissal. The jury then pinned a single count on her. Iva Toguri became the first American woman convicted of treason. Sentenced to ten years, she served six behind bars and was released in 1956. No one else who participated in the radio broadcasts was ever incarcerated or even charged.

In 1977, some journalists dug up evidence that the government had coached and threatened two of the major witnesses against her in the trial, and President Ford issued her an unconditional pardon. The notorious Tokyo Rose has lived quietly in Chicago ever since, working in a family gift shop.

We think Hollywood should pay Iva big bucks to make a movie of her story. It could be directed by Jane Fonda (Hanoi Jane) another woman who became the object of a collective need to blame women during wars.

"ROSIE THE RIVETER"
THE SONG THAT
STARTED IT ALL:
LYRICS BY REDD
EVANS AND JOHN
JACOB LOEB,
MUSIC BY KAY KYSER

All the day long,
Whether rain
or shine,
She's a part of
the assembly line.
She's making
history,
Working for
victory,
Rosie the Riveter.

Keeps a sharp
lookout for
sabatoge,
Sitting up there
on the fuselage.
That little girl will
do more than a
male will do.

Rosie the Riveter

Funny how war changes things, usually for the worst. But here's an aspect of one war, World War II, that created positive changes forever for working women in America.

In that global war effort, all able-bodied young men were called up for service in the military. Overnight, there was no one left to do a man's job...except, of course, the women. Many girls donned coveralls and hard hats and went to work welding battleships, riveting airplane wings, and working behind the scenes within the military. For the duration the war, macho chauvinism had to keep its mouth shut while women performed jobs they'd never been allowed to do before! And guess what...they worked every bit as hard as the guys before them. Some jobs they even did better! Because of their size they could work in tighter spots. They proved that women were capable of entering the building and industrial trades that had formerly been closed to them.

Rosie the Riveter by J. Howard Miller
National Archives

More than seven million working women broke out of conventional female roles in support of the war effort. Collectively, they became a new stereotype nicknamed Rosie the Riveter after a 1942 song composed by bandleader Kay Kyser. His song paid homage to a worker from Long Island, Rosalind Walker. The idea of Rosie caught on and was disseminated by the war propaganda machine. In 1943, Rosie was given a face by two different illustrators. Each was based on a real-life war worker whose first name happened to be Rose. J. Howard Miller's image was of Rose Bonavita Hickey, who set a record at the General Motors Eastern Aircraft Division by completing 3,345 rivets on a torpedo bomber in less than six hours. Norman Rockwell's Rosie was inspired by Rose Will Monroe, a worker in the Willow Run Aircraft Factory in Ypsilanti, Michigan. Walter Pigeon discovered her while doing scouting for a government film to promote war bonds. She appeared in a number of such movies.

But conditions weren't rosy for all these Rosies. One out of 10, or 600,000, women were African-American. These women encountered the same prejudice black men did before the war: They were given the hardest, least-skilled, lowest-paying jobs solely on account of their color. Nevertheless, the war empowered women of color to enter the larger world of labor. Previously they had been resigned to work as domestics.

After the war the guys came back and Rosies were asked to give up their jobs and go back to the kitchen. Some did. Others, like Rose Will Monroe, couldn't, because their husbands were dead and they had children to support. Nevertheless, most of these Rosies were either laid off or lost their seniority. The women who continued to work were

Rosie the Riveter by Norman Rockwell. By permission of the Norman Rockwell Family Agency. Copyright © 1943 The Norman Rockwell Family Entities

NAZI VALLEY GIRL BIKER CHICK FLORENCE NIGHTINGALE AUNT JEMIMA FLAPPER CARMEN MIRANDA MOTHER TERESA TOKYO ROSE

refused promotions and often moved into lower-paying jobs. Rose Monroe drove a taxi, operated a beauty salon, and finally started her own construction company.

But the country had become accustomed to seeing women do jobs formerly reserved for men. And women got used to earning good money for their labor. The era of Rosie the Riveter ushered in the concept of equal pay for equal work. And it paved the way for women and people of color to later enter trade and construction unions that had been exclusively white and male. Rosie the Riveter was one stereotype that had lasting ramifications in the areas of women's rights, civil rights, and labor politics.

Lolita

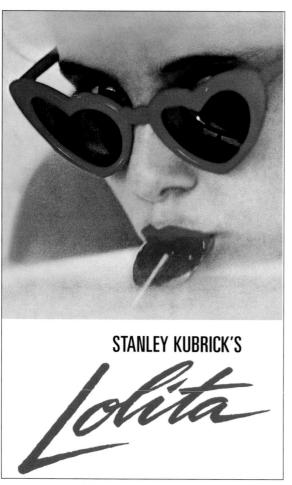

STANLEY KUBRICK'S

Lolita

Poster for Stanley Kubrick's film. © 1961 Turner entertainment Co., an AOL Time Warner company

In 1955, émigré writer Vladimir Nabokov published the novel *Lolita*, which became an overnight scandal in the U.S. It was the story of Humbert Humbert, a 40-year-old college professor obsessed with a prepubescent 12-year-old girl, Dolores "Lolita" Haze. Humbert goes so far as to marry Lolita's mother just to be near her daughter. When Mom conveniently dies, he makes his move and takes the bereaved child on a sex-filled road trip. He is in heaven until she runs away into the arms of another older man. It sounds like a sad story all around, but Nabokov manages to make it into a comedy, a farce. We are enticed to look into Humbert's perverted soul because Nabokov makes him so ridiculous and deluded.

Lolita was a sensation, earning both praise and damnation. No one could keep their minds off *Lolita* and its theme of sex and adolescent girls. In 1961, Stanley Kubrick made a film, with Nabokov himself writing the screenplay and James Mason and Sue Lyon in the leading roles. The Catholic Legion of Decency forbade church members to see it.

Lolita became a stereotype: a seductive adolescent girl, a nymphet ready to have unlimited sex with older men. Do an Internet search under Lolita and up pops an endless barrage of porno sites featuring supposed underage girls.

But the Lolita stereotype is based on a misreading of Nabokov's novel which, despite the title, is really the story of a murdering pedophile, not of his victim. Lolita is a captive, subjected to all the standard threats and tricks pedophiles use to entrap children. She runs away as soon as she can, but unfortunately into the arms of another man like Humbert. Lolita redeems herself with an early marriage and pregnancy—and there the book leaves her, with no hint about her ultimate fate. But Humbert's story is complete: He self-implodes of a heart attack while facing trial for the murder of the man who took Lolita from him. Nabokov's novel is curiously moral, some might say uplifting: Both abusers die and the victim lives. By novel's end, we cannot be sure that Lolita's libido wasn't just a figment of Humbert's wildly lecherous imagination.

Nabokov's story struck a chord among middle-aged men who lust after young girls. But we think it's curious that Lolita is the stereotype that grew from the book, based on grown men's fantasies that teenage girls "want" them, when it should have been Humbert, the creepy pedophile. We could use a Humbert stereotype to help young girls and boys identify dangerous grown-ups, but instead we have, ingrained in society, Lolita, one more sex-crazed girl who's "gotta have it."

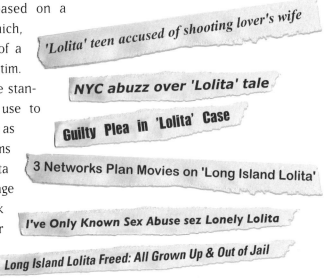

'Lolita' teen accused of shooting lover's wife

NYC abuzz over 'Lolita' tale

Guilty Plea in 'Lolita' Case

3 Networks Plan Movies on 'Long Island Lolita'

I've Only Known Sex Abuse sez Lonely Lolita

Long Island Lolita Freed: All Grown Up & Out of Jail

Life Calms Down for Characters in Long Island Lolita Drama

BOY, DID THE MEDIA (above) GET THIS ONE WRONG! Amy Fisher was a 16-year-old Long Island high-school student who shot her 38-year-old boyfriend's wife in 1992. She went to prison for seven years. The only thing the Long Island Lolita had in common with Nabokov's Lolita was that both were harassed by middle-aged men who should have been getting it somewhere else. Why isn't Joey Buttafuoco the Hempstead Humbert?

Bra Burner/ Feminazi

The image of the Bra Burner, a man-hating feminist who tears off her brassiere and throws it into a bonfire to cast off the yoke of patriarchy, is firmly etched in the memory of every American over 40. There's only one problem: Bra burning never happened.

Here's the scoop: In 1968, at the height of the Vietnam War, a group of feminists organized a protest at the Miss America Pageant in Atlantic City. They held placards declaring "Let's Judge Ourselves as People." They tossed all sorts of female accessories like makeup, high heels, and girdles into a trash can. A photo of feminist leader Robin Morgan tossing a bra into the mix found its way into the press. A reporter for the *New York Post*, sent to do a humorous piece on the protest, likened the act to antiwar protests where draft cards were burned in front of TV cameras. In fact, no bra was ever torched, but the public liked the idea of women burning their underwear and has kept it alive ever since. Generally the Bra Burner stereotype is used to discredit and trivialize the women's movement.

Unfortunately, every era needs to demonize feminists. The Feminazi was the 1990s version. The term was coined by radio talk-show host Rush Limbaugh to describe women who support abortion rights. It was taken up by ultra-right-wing conservatives everywhere and came to refer to feminists in general. Twenty years after the women's movement changed American society forever, the old stereotypes like Bra Burner began to seem too tame.

A Feminazi is a strident, controlling bitch who—Oh, horrible crime!—insists on equal rights for women. She doesn't agree with the right-wing construct that the man is the ruler of the home. Her goal in life is to turn men into whimpering slaves who take care of the kids and share the housecleaning, something men must resist at all costs or American society will crumple even more. The Guerrilla Girls are still waiting for the day when everyone will think of the Feminist as a positive stereotype. Don't let us wait too long.

This is what a bra looked like in 1968? Who wouldn't want to burn it, even though no one did?

Robin Morgan, organizer of September 1968 demonstration against the Miss America Pageant, tosses a bra into the "Freedom Trash Can" on the boardwalk in Atlantic City. It was the first protest of the contemporary feminist movement.

Valley Girl

Being a Valley Girl is first and foremost about shopping. Teenagers—particularly insecure young girls who are preyed upon by the fashion industry and will do anything to look right and get approval—are primary targets of marketing aces who want them to spend big bucks in shopping malls. Here's a letter we received from one of the original Valley Girls:

A way long time ago, in 1980, this totally awesome-to-the-max shopping mall, The Galleria, was out like in the Valley. It was a super bitchin place to go and I mean like when you weren't getting your toenails done or your braces fixed, you could just go there and like check out all the Mega Buff Valley Dudes who hung out. Swishy BuFu guys were Okay 'cause they dressed right outta GQ but there weren't any skanky freaks around the mall to barf you out..

Some of my friends were like so totally ku-el that some daughter of Slimeball Retard, Frank Mega-Gross Zappa, wrote a song to make her Dad's grody-to-the-max career get all noisy again. Had a gross-me-out name like Moon, not a 'xlent one like Heather, Brittany, or Barbi! She trashed us, made us out like total space cadets, air heads, crispos, Jell-O-brains. I mean gag me with a spoon! Kiss my tuna! Like we didn't have anything happening inside our fluffy 'dos? Fer shurr, we were mega-shoppers and really cute babes but, you tell me what was like more important in 1982? Duh, remember who was president?

Whatever. Like, if we were such grodies, why did they make so many tubular movies about us like Valley Girl and Fast Times at Ridgemont High? And those totally cosmic articles in wicked newspapers outta' New York and Washington about how we invented Mallspeak. And then like, hello, there were Vals like us all over the country! Build a mall, get some Valley Girls!

The Galleria is like gone, it got swallowed up in the earthquake. Totally. But malls are everywhere now! Us original Vals are grown up and have like kids and strollers and stuff. But we still drive to the mall for everything! It's like the American way of life! Our daughters grow up to be Valley Girls, too. Shopping and being totally obsessed with your clothes and appearance is good, clean fun. And patriotic, too! A ditz with a credit card is a girl who will stay out of serious trouble... until she maxes it out and has to do something really yukky like sell sex or drugs to get outta debt. Ohmigod fer shurr.

Love ya,
Stacie, Encino, California, in like 2003

PETER **FONDA**   NANCY **SINATRA**   BRUCE **DERN**   DIANE **LADD**

THE WILD ANGELS

THEIR CREDO IS **VIOLENCE!**
THEIR GOD IS **HATE!**

Biker Chicks then

Biker Chick

It's hard to talk about Biker Chicks without starting with Bikers, who got their outlaw image on July 4, 1947, at an American Motorcycle Association rally in Hollister, California. Too big from the beginning (Bikers nearly outnumbered the townspeople), it was soon out of control. Races took place spontaneously in the middle of Main Street. Cyclists drove their motorcycles right into bars. Outrageous behavior and numerous injuries occurred during the four-day event, but there was no rioting, looting, or violence. A report noted that one out of every ten attendees was female. The girls wore tight sweaters and slacks and rode on the back of the guys' bikes. A photographer from *Time* took a staged photo of a drunk on a bike, and the image of Bikers—and their "old ladies"—as fuck-you hedonists, out to break all society's rules, was created.

The film *The Wild One* (1953), with Marlon Brando, was based on the rally. A slew of "bikesploitation" flicks followed: *The Wild Angels, The Glory Stompers,* and later, *The Cycle Savages,* and *Easy Rider.* A love interest was a must, and presto, the Biker Chick was born. The posters tell it all: She was a young, beautiful, sexpot hanging off the back of a bike, keeping a man warm at night.

Biker clubs and gangs sprang up to embody the Biker stereotype. Sometimes for real and sometimes just for show, they are still going strong today. Any club worth its wheels has a beauty pageant to promote the Biker Chick ideal. This pageant chick, also immortalized in the Biker magazines, is tall, with long straight hair and huge, perhaps surgically enhanced, breasts. Posed in leather lingerie on a big machine, she's usually surrounded by groups of today's Bikers, average age over 50, with graying ponytails and beer bellies. She's a fantasy: Who could ride a bike dressed like that?

However, if a Biker Chick is any female who gets on a bike, there have been some significant improvements to the stereotype. For one, there are lots of all-female bike clubs whose members are riders, not passengers. The Devil Dolls publish a calender with pictures of themselves posing alongside their machines. They ain't nothing like the Biker Chicks in movies and magazines. Neither are the women who race motorcycles, some against male competitors. And let's not forget Dykes on Bikes, the beloved group of Lesbians who ride in every Gay Pride parade. They have a passion for their bikes and for confounding hetero stereotypes.

Biker Chicks now

FOR CENTURIES, A WOMAN'S MOST IMPORTANT OCCUPATION WAS to find the right mate and have children. This quest is complicated nowadays because a girl also has to find a good job—not just for her life before having kids, but for her entire life. Stereotypes follow her on this search, both at home and on the job. Here are a few standouts.

Women's work is never done:
Find mate, be Supermom, gt gd job, have fun

Debutante/ Socialite

Debs are young women from prominent families who are "presented" en masse at an elaborate ball, around their 18th birthdays. Although the event is all very discreet and understated, it is, in fact, a mating ritual, as overt as any rite in traditional societies. The Deb wears a white gown to represent her virginal state. The big moment comes when she processes across a stage, faces the crowd in all her finery, and gives a deep, sweeping curtsy. This shows her grace, humility, the size of her parents' bank account, and perhaps a bit of cleavage. Then everyone gets tanked, and stories swirl for years to

The pleasure of your company
is requested
at a conspicuously extravagant event
sponsored by a bunch of social climbers
to imitate mating rituals
of European Aristocrats
in the fervent desire
that their virginal daughters
date and marry
men from the right kind of background

Debutante ball © Bettmann/Corbis

come about what really happened after the ball.

Stereotypically, Debs are WASPs with long, blonde hair. They are thin, well groomed, and fashionably, but not too provocatively, dressed. They possess good table manners, can converse indefinitely without ever stating an idea or opinion, and write terrific thank-you notes. They ride horses, play golf and tennis, and go to the same prep schools and colleges that their parents did. Sometimes they take their horses with them. Debs are taught not to hang out with people, especially guys, unlike themselves.

Debs are supposed to work a bit, marry well, and become Socialite wives. Socialites keep themselves busy breeding and maintaining the proper social connections. After their children are in school, they do volunteer work for high-profile charities and get their pictures in newspapers with men in tuxedos. They are mentioned in Society columns if they do something noteworthy or naughty. Through it all, it is crucial that they stay really skinny, "Social X rays," as Tom Wolfe described them in *Bonfire of the Vanities.* Jacqueline Kennedy was a good example of a Deb/Socialite until she broke rank and began a career as a book editor.

Today's Deb balls are no longer the exclusive province of the WASP establishment. Cotillions exist across the U.S., especially in the South, organized by striving parents who want their children to learn the behavior of heterosexual aristocrats. Ethnic groups formerly excluded from Debutante balls now hold their own, and aspire to the ideal that well-bred, well-trained women get the best husbands. African-American and Polish-American Deb balls emphasize education and making it, rather than the old WASP idea of already being there. And then there are the Drag Balls that take the Deb Ball/Cotillion stereotype of "coming out" to hilarious extremes. Check out the Magnolia Cotillion in New Orleans.

Gold Digger

A Gold Digger is a woman whose ambition is to find a rich husband. "Gold Digger" was a Flapper-era term first used in the 1920s to describe a modern woman who pursued a man, known as the Gold Mine, for his money. A guy who did the same with women was a Forty-Niner. The female stereotype stuck, but the lighthearted Flapper humor got lost. Every family seems to have to cope with at least one Gold Digger. No woman wants to cop to being one, even if she is.

A Gold Digger is not all that different from a Deb in that they are both looking for wealthy husbands. But a Gold Digger comes from a lower social class and will marry any man for his money, be he 18 or 80. (Hey, it's not a bad deal: Anna Nicole Smith inherited millions from an octogenarian she met at a strip club, then married. He died nine months later.)

Both Broadway and Hollywood love Gold Diggers. *Gentlemen Prefer Blondes,* about the fortune-hunting exploits of Lorelei Lee and Dorothy, started out as a novel by Anita Loos in 1925. It was so popular that Loos transformed it into a play (1925), a musical (1949), and a film twice (1928, and the 1953 version with Marilyn Monroe and Jane Russell). Busby Berkeley's *Gold Diggers of 1933* featured a chorus line of girls dressed as coins. On celluloid, the Gold Digger became a sexy, young, blonde showgirl on the make for a rich,

"We're in the Money"—the opening number of Busby Berkeley's film *Gold Diggers of 1933*

usually older, man. She was a descendant of the Femme Fatale/Vamp but hardly an evil vampire. Instead of sucking a man's blood, she offered him happiness, sex, and the opportunity to dominate her in exchange for a life of security and luxury. She was kind, lovable, perhaps a little dim, and clearly unable to provide for herself in the fashion to which she aspired. Marilyn Monroe specialized in Gold Digger roles, most notably in *How to Marry a Millionaire* and *Gentlemen Prefer Blondes.* Gold Diggers mirrored the cultural cliché that when men search for a mate, they are interested in what she looks like, and women, in turn, want to know how much money he makes.

Trophy Wife

Now that 25 percent of U.S. wives earn more than their husbands, the Gold Digger seems a little stale. Enter the Trophy Wife, the contemporary, liberated woman who, despite her own career success, still wants a guy even more successful. In 1989, an article in *Fortune* magazine identified a growing phenomenon among wealthy middle-aged male executives who had dumped their first wives. As a group, these CEOs displayed a tendency to pick a very different kind of mate the second time around.

As explained in *Fortune:* "In some cases [the exec] with the old, nice, matronly wife is looked down on. He's not keeping up with appearances. Enter the second wife: a decade or two younger... sometimes several inches taller, beautiful and very often accomplished. The second wife certifies her husband's status and...she dispels the notion that men peak sexually at age 18....Powerful men are beginning to demand trophy wives."

The exec works long hours. So does his Trophy Wife. That way his alimony and child support payments don't bite too deeply into their extravagant lifestyle. They don't have children because he's already been down that road, but she does have her hands full with the resentment from the children of his first marriage. The happy couple loves to be seen and photographed at charity benefits and movie premieres. A Trophy Wife is only half of this team, but as usual the stereotype is directed at her, not him, even though he's surely her Trophy Husband, too.

Hollywood, that stereotype factory, has given us its own spin on the Trophy Mate Syndrome, one not so far from the reality of the Trophy Wife. One film critic calls it "Beauty and the Gheez," the endless slew of movies where aging male stars are paired with gorgeous actresses half their age (see list at left). "I'm sure the average 50-year-old woman does not want to see a movie about a 20-year-old woman and a man her husband's age, and I doubt that the 20-year-old woman wants to see that either," says culture critic Katha Pollitt. But in real life, many of these male actors have young Trophy Wives. So do many movie executives. Need we say more?

It was worth the price of admission just to see Jack Nicholson in bed with a woman his own age.
—A 60-something movie-goer commenting on *About Schmidt,* the 2002 film.

Left: Gwyneth Paltrow kisses Michael Douglas in *A Perfect Murder.*
Far left: Wendy Deng marries media mogul Rupert Murdoch in 1999.

Soccer Mom

Everyone has an idea of who a Soccer Mom is: a youngish, educated, heterosexual, married, middle- or upper-middle-class white woman with school-age or younger children. She drives an SUV or minivan. She lives in the suburbs and probably doesn't have an outside job. In fact, her job, which she does fabulously well, is her children. She is part coach, part referee, part confidant, and full-time chauffeur, since the 'burbs are built around gasoline consumption.

A Soccer Mom has a traditional marriage. Her husband is the breadwinner and since he's away from home a lot, she manages the household and the kids. This stay-at-home mom used to be the norm, or at least the ideal, for almost every social class, but today she is an endangered species, comprising less than 12 percent of the population. She is as likely to drive her daughter as her son to sports practice—soccer being a sport played by both girls and boys. Football, Wrestling, or Rugby Mom just doesn't cut it in this post-feminist age.

The Soccer Mom appeared on the scene in the late 1980s, concurrent with the growing interest in soccer in the U.S. By 1996, "Soccer Mom" was declared the term of the year by the American Dialect Society. That same year, Soccer Moms were considered a crucial voting block in the Clinton/Dole election and were courted by both Democrat and Republicans. Remember who won the Soccer Moms? Clinton. And who won their husbands' vote? Dole. Hmmmmmm. Soccer Moms also are credited with organizing protests like the Million Mom March against gun violence. Go Soccer Moms!

Stage Mom

One hundred and fifty years ago, an actress or entertainer was considered no better than a prostitute. To be the mother of one was almost as great a disgrace. But the birth of the modern entertainment industry changed all that. With the promise of celebrity and wads of money, parents fell all over themselves to promote the stage and screen careers of their talented sons and daughters, the latter as preadolescent beauty queens, athletes, actresses—even as teenage Playboy Bunnies.

Granted, there are good and bad Stage Moms, but the bad one is the stereotype. She's pushy, overbearing, and manipulates her child's career with little concern for the kid's well-being. Stage Mothers often wanted to be in showbiz themselves, but gave it up to marry and have children. A Stage Mother lives through her child, and when that child is female there can also be an envy that manifests itself in cruelty and abuse. The child exists to redeem the mother's thwarted ambition and, in the process, is robbed of a childhood.

As early as 1933, Hollywood made a movie entitled *Stage Mother* with Maureen O'Sullivan playing a Stage Mom who sees the light and saves her child. One of the most successful and often-performed musicals, *Gypsy*, is based on the real life of the famous entertainer Gypsy Rose Lee, whose Stage Mother turned her into a stripper. There is a long list of entertainers rumored to have had cruel Stage Mothers: Jean Harlow, Judy Garland, Natalie Wood, Maria Callas, Brooke Shields, and Drew Barrymore.

Mothers get the bad rap, but there should be an evil Stage Father stereotype, too. Kit Culkin, father of Macaulay and Kieran, forced his kids into showbiz and was eventually kicked out of the family. Joe Jackson, father of Michael, Janet, LaToya, etc., was rumored to be exceptionally hard on his performing kids. And there have always been the Sports Dads who live through their kid's athletic accomplishments and sometimes abuse them if they lose.

You rarely hear about the good Stage Moms, but one example is the mother of young mogul Melissa Joan Hart, who produces *Sabrina, the Teenage Witch*, her daughter's show. "Mother Managers" is what *Ebony* magazine called the moms of child actors Tisha Campbell, Kadeem Hardison, and Malcolm-Jamal Warner in a 1993 article. We've also recently heard the term "Momagers." That sounds a lot more appropriate today than Stage Mom, now that kids themselves beg to be in showbiz and parents, by law, can't cheat them out of all their money like they used to do in the old days; they have to manage it instead.

Diva/Prima Donna

Diva, from the Latin for "divine goddess," is a female singer who's larger than life and demands special treatment. She has extraordinary talent, legions of fans, and sycophant staffers who cater to her every need—the more ridiculous the better. The flip side of the Diva is her fundamental insecurity and vulnerability: She needs constant fawning over in order to deliver a spectacular performance. If she doesn't get it, or if her career goes down the toilet, she succumbs to depression, drugs...even suicide.

Great opera stars like Maria Callas were the first modern Divas. Later came the pop stars: Diana Ross, Mariah Carey, Whitney Houston. To be called a Diva is more a compliment than an insult, because Diva status is only conferred on the greatest of the great.

A Prima Donna, short for *prima donna assoluta*, is the principal female singer in an opera, or, by extension, anyone who is temperamental and self-important, like a Diva. No one wants to be called a Prima Donna because it implies that you are arrogant beyond your right to be. You don't have to be a singer to be a Prima Donna. You don't even have to be a woman: The term is increasingly used to describe difficult male performers and even star athletes like basketball and tennis players.

The historic model for the Diva and Prima Donna was probably not a woman at all, but the temperamental 17th- and 18th-century castrati. At that time in Europe, women were forbidden, by papal decree, to sing sacred music in public. The Catholic Church figured out a clever way around the prohibition: Cut the testicles off boys as young as seven to keep their voices from deepening as they matured. When these castrati reached adulthood, they retained a remarkable singing range thanks to their large male lung capacity combined with their high alto soprano pitch. Castrati possessed extraordinary, otherworldly voices unattainable by either male or female. Between 1600 and 1750, 70 percent of all opera singers were castrati. Sought after throughout Europe, they were the first stars of

DIVA ON BOARD

- According to the book *Molto Agitato*, Kathleen Battle, former Metropolitan Opera soprano, insisted that all communication go through her manager. One day, as Battle was being chauffeured to a performance, she telephoned her manager and asked her to call the limo driver and tell him to turn down the air-conditioning.

Famed Castrati Senesino (far left) and Gaetano Berenstadt (far right) perform a Handel opera.

Western music, kind of like rock stars of today. They were notoriously difficult, often demanding roles to be specifically written or rewritten for them, and even engaging in improvised competitive feats on stage to prove their extraordinary abilities. The last recorded castrato, Alessandro Moreschi, director of the Sistine Chapel choir, died in 1922.

Did the first female opera singers model their Diva behavior on the castrati who preceded them as superstars? Or does great singing simply beget Divas?

Supermodel

Once upon a time, the clothes were the stars and the models were just bodies to hang them on. They weren't household names. In the 1950s and early 1960s a few models were known by name, such as Jean Simmons and Verushka. Then, starting in the late 1960s, models became stars. First there was Twiggy, whose big eyes, long legs, and emaciated physique ushered in the Mod miniskirt look. A few years later, gap-toothed Lauren Hutton became the first "imperfect" or individual-looking model, a trend that continues today. Who had the idea to market models as commodities, as brand names? Was it agents like Ford, Elite, and Casablanca? Was it managers and lawyers, who took their cue from their movie and rock-star clients? We'll never know for sure, although it's a good bet that it wasn't the models themselves, who were usually teenagers when they were "discovered" and catapulted from small towns the world over to New York, London, Paris, or Milan. Suddenly, it wasn't enough to be a model; you had to be a Supermodel.

A Supermodel's income ratcheted up to fit her exalted status. Papparazzi followed her around from after-party to after-after-party. Rock stars wanted to date her. She received marriage proposals from fans all over the world. She was expected to be difficult and demanding—a fashion Diva. She was thought to be dumb, but how dumb is it to earn $40 million by the time you are 30, like Claudia Schiffer?

Of course, now that there are legions of Supermodels, the term has become almost meaningless. We bet Tyra, Christy, Rebecca, Cindy, Kathy, Amber, etc. wish there was a new stereotype to set them off from their lesser colleagues. Any ideas?

Female Exec/ Lady Boss

Thirty-five years ago, a female college grad went to work as a secretary, while her male counterpart became a management trainee. Then feminists forced corporations to hire and promote women to executive positions. Men were angry about being bossed by a woman. To assuage those fears, Female Execs acted like "one of the boys": they donned power suits, talked tough, and learned to play golf. That worked pretty well, but didn't erase the myths and misconceptions that cast the Female Exec as an imposing, scary woman who works long hours and is a horrible Bitch when she has her period. If she was single, the Lady Boss was even more scary because her whole life was her job. If she had a husband or partner and kids, she was seen as not focused enough on work. She also was thought to be too emotional and lacking the self-confidence needed to get to the top.

Today, according to the Bureau of Labor Statistics, women are 33 percent of business school grads and hold 49 percent of the managerial positions in corporations, up from 15 percent in 1968. But the myths persist, preventing women from breaking the glass ceiling: There are only four female CEOs in the Fortune 500 and a total of only eight in the Fortune 1000. Women in managerial and professional positions earn 29 percent less than their male counterparts.

The good news: Women are bringing their own management style to the executive suite. They no longer feel they have to act just like the guys, and they are starting to be appreciated for their skills. Studies have repeatedly shown that women execs are superior to male execs by almost every measure. And these were studies designed to evaluate executives, not to find gender differences; women's higher scores were revealed in the data analyses, surprising researchers. Some executives say they're beginning to develop a new hiring bias. According to *BusinessWeek*, "If forced to choose between equally qualified male and female candidates for a top-level job, they say they often pick the woman...because they believe she will do a better job."

Brent Clark, the CEO of footcare chain Pell Inc., chooses women over men because he thinks they are more reliable, less territorial, and excel at "all sorts of intangibles that can help an organization." Anu Shukla, who founded Rubric Inc., says, "I would rather hire a woman. I know I'm going to get a certain quality of work, I know I'm going to get a certain dedication."

Time for a new stereotype: Female Exec as consummate team player and leader of a happier, more productive staff.

Anchorwoman

They dress alike. They talk alike. They have the same hairdo no matter what their race or ethnic background. They have no identifiable regional or ethnic accents. They are our nation's Anchorwomen. They sit behind the desks at local stations and national newsmagazines, but they're not allowed on the major networks' nightly news shows—TV's glass ceiling—except as weekend subs.

An Anchorwoman might be an exceptional journalist, or she might be a Bimbo recruited for her eye appeal. In either case, almost all the fan mail she receives is about her clothes and hairstyle, hardly ever about her news reports. And when she's old and not so cute anymore, it's out the door, replaced by a younger version.

When Marciarose Shestack, the first woman to anchor a big-city primetime news show, tried to get her first anchor gig in 1960, she was told, "Over my dead body," by the station's general manager. "He, like others, believed that women were not authority figures, they do not have good voices, and the audience would not accept them as credible communicators of world events," Shestack said. Things are better today, as long as a woman is young and attractive. A 44-year-old Hartford, Connecticut, Anchorwoman was awarded $8 million a few years ago after suing the station she claimed fired her because of age and gender discrimination. Most older Anchorwomen just try to look younger than they are. Fox's Greta Van Susteren, and many others, have gotten face-lifts to stay in the game. Watch the news tonight and see if you can find an Anchorwoman with expression lines on her forehead. We found them on male anchors, but not on the women. Botox anyone?

The nation's Anchorwomen: The names and faces might be different, but the hair stays the same.

83

Chapter Six

Race and religion:
Presenting our own ethnic doll collection

WHEN WE GOT TO thinking about religious and ethnic stereotypes, we found them all so exaggerated and ridiculous we realized one way to disarm them would be to toy with them a bit. So the Guerrilla Girls are proud to present a new line of playthings...to have, to hold, and to let go of, faithfully handcrafted in the good old U.S. of A. We guarantee that at least one of these dolls will make you feel superior, no matter what your ethnic group.

Lauren, Jewish American Princess

Lauren's wealthy parents have treated her like royalty since the day she was born, and she expects you to do the same. Lauren is high maintenance and high cost: She wants lots of material things and does she know how to get them! Lauren is not one of those girls who suffer from low self-esteem!

Lauren comes with a collection of shopping bags from every top fashion designer, a datebook that includes weekly hair and nail appointments, and a retractable nose job with three different and unique variations. She's programmed with an adorable selection of Jewish Princess jokes. Example: "What does a Jewish Princess make for dinner? Reservations."

Now we know there are feminist historians who've said, "The JAP stereotype is no less offensive just because the idea of the Jew as 'money-grubbing, conniving, selfish, malicious, and untrustworthy' has been updated and put into a skirt." But we say, lighten up, historians, maybe you just need to go shopping!

At 30, Lauren turns into a JEWISH MOTHER (sold separately), programmed with many familiar and endearing exclamations including "Ach, don't worry about me!" and "You're too busy to call your mother?"

Because of popular demand from other ethnic groups, Lauren also comes in BAP (Black American Princess), CAP (Chinese American Princess), and IAP (Italian American Princess), all fully accessorized.

Theresa, the Good Catholic Girl

Theresa carries around so much guilt that we've hidden a button under her school uniform that, when pushed, apologizes for everything, including world poverty! Theresa is obedient, loyal, self-effacing, suffering, dignified, and respectful.

But take off that plaid uniform, make sure her parents aren't around, and Terry will do anything, ANYTHING that a male (boyfriend or priest) asks her! Lay her down and she becomes a convenient doormat for her husband forever, since her religion forbids divorce.

Also available in virginal, white Communion dress to remind her that even at seven, she's the bride of Christ! Comes in Asian-American, Latina, and African-American versions with hair and complexion to match.

WARNING: Due to a manufacturing flaw related to real-life Catholics in the U.S., 97 percent of Theresa dolls will use contraceptives sometime in their lives and 87 percent will make up their own minds about having an abortion. Some dolls may even join rebellious Catholic groups like Dignity or turn into Lesbians! Sorry, no returns or refunds.

Running Dear, Indian Princess

Running Dear is the young and favorite daughter of an Indian chief, a noble among the savages. She is beautiful, modest, soft-spoken, and courageous. She wears a scanty buckskin tunic that falls off her shoulder from time to time to remind us that Indian princesses do not need cumbersome Western underwear. And she's perfectly willing to aid the forces that want to destroy her people or put them on reservations.

Running Dear knows how to hunt, put up tepees, and lead expedition parties through the wilderness. She can teach white men how to survive the long, cold winter and will even risk her life to save the one she loves.

This doll wears a small crucifix necklace to remind you that she will forsake her people and convert to Christianity if asked by a white man who wants to make her his squaw. If Running Dear marries this white guy, you can exchange her for the second doll in our Native American series, Squaw With No Name (not pictured). However, if Running Dear decides not to marry, you must exchange her for Corn Maiden (not pictured), who stays with her people, raises a large extended family, has an important position in tribal government, and perhaps even becomes chief.

Pearl, China Doll

Pearl is every man's dream come true! She's beautiful, exotic, and eager to please. Her meekness and obedience are legendary. Pearl is ready to replace any troublesome and demanding Caucasian wives! She comes with one native costume, which can be traded for many American-style outfits. You may have heard that, statistically, Asian wives are not more accommodating than Anglo ones, but don't worry, that doesn't apply to our Pearl.

This doll also comes in a Sumiko the Geisha variety, which is a little more expensive because a Geisha Girl is a highly trained entertainer. While she might have started out as an orphan or deserted child, after a long apprenticeship she's in business, selling her talents, one by one. She'd never think of committing herself to a single man! She'd lose too much money!

Madame X, Dragon Lady

Aggressive and scheming, this doll will keep you bewitched and bewildered for hours! Unlike Pearl who kills with kindness, Madame X just kills. She'll seduce you and then sell you down the river. All this without a shred of remorse or a second glance through those inscrutable slit eyes and her expressionless face. We based Madame X's personality on characters from Hollywood movies and TV, like Ling in *Ally McBeal*, and the wives of Asian dictators.

Madame X comes with a slinky Chinese-style silk dress with a deep slit up the side. Instead of the bound feet that kept her ancestors in line, she wears a different podiatric encumbrance: stiletto heels.

Rosa, Hot Tamale

Rosa is a hot-blooded Latina who loves to dance to loud salsa music. She is short and has dark hair and a fiery disposition. Push her hidden buttons and she's in your face, ready to engage in a verbal fist fight before you can say "Arroz y Frijoles!" Rosa has a passionate and flirtatious nature, which makes all the Anglo boys think she's easy. But mess with her and her macho father, together with all her brothers and cousins, will be on your case in a nanosecond!

Rosa's family might be poor, but they all work hard and help provide for each other. Maybe this explains why Latinas are starting their own businesses at a rate four times faster than the rest of the population!

Tiffany, the Foxy Flygirl

Tiffany is thin, with long legs, firm and luscious breasts, and buns of steel. Tiffany is very, very sexy and seductive. Her features are kinda white. She wears provocative clothes of leather and lace and has six-inch fingernails. She works her attributes better than white or Asian girls! Men who fall for her cannot help themselves: she's a Vamp.

Tiffany has the look adopted by many African-American women, and white women, too, who make it in the entertainment or fashion world. She's fun to play with, but if you don't watch her carefully, she will take up with dangerous men and get into BIG trouble!

Sapphire, Matriarch and Church Lady

Fashioned after the character created for the *Amos 'N' Andy* show, Sapphire is a tough-minded, head-strong, no-nonsense lady with ideas of her own that she's not afraid to share with the rest of the world. Any back talk and she'll hit you upside the head. She's been taught to defer to whites, but to African-American males she's a terror! She constantly out-wits them with the help of her sister-hood of church ladies just like her. She knows the comings and goings of everyone in the neighborhood and has an opinion of their behavior, too! Sapphire doesn't have a male compan-ion doll because we couldn't find one who would put up with her.

Comes with voice box for her constant "runnin' at the mouth" and dress-up Sunday clothes including a big hat and pocketbook.

Latisha, the Welfare Queen

WARNING: THE MAJORITY OF WELFARE RECIPIENTS HAVE ALWAYS BEEN WHITE, BUT, DUE TO POPULAR DEMAND, LATISHA IS BLACK.

Poor Latisha! She's unemployed, overweight, and so lazy it takes all the energy she can muster just to watch TV all day and eat junk food! But she's a Queen because she's figured out how to get you and me to pay all her bills through the welfare department! Latisha believes in diversity, too. Every one of her six children has a different father! She also practices deficit spending: She buys everything on the layaway plan and, in the end, pays twice as much.

Latisha was expressly created for us by Ronald Reagan, who coined the term "Welfare Queen" in one of his speeches. Hurry and place your order because due to the new welfare laws, Latisha no longer exists. Updated Post Welfare version comes with two full-time jobs, high blood pressure, and diabetes, as well as several teenage children in serious trouble 'cause they're home alone day and night.

Scheherazade, the Harem Girl

She's a curvy, bare-naveled Muslim woman who lives in either a lantern or a harem. The lantern model, when rubbed, appears and disappears to grant wishes. The harem model is one of many wives of a rich and mysterious sheik. She spends all day lounging around with the other wives, hoping to be chosen as the sex object for the night! In her free time she does belly dancing and peels grapes.

We based Scheherazade on paintings by 19th-century European artists like Delacroix and Ingres, and on the 1970s TV series, *I Dream of Jeannie.*

Scheherazade wears a halter top, harem pants and a sexy veil that reveals more than it hides. Accessories include toe rings, tons of eye makeup, and heavy jewelry that makes noise when you move her.

Nizreen, the Good Muslim Wife

Unfortunate Nizreen! Her father couldn't find a rich man to marry her so he shipped her out to a fundamentalist who keeps her silent, repressed, invisible, and illiterate! Practically all you can see of her under those robes are her sad, sad eyes! She would never dream of demanding an education, a job, or any rights at all. But she does dream of having a son or daughter who will become a suicide bomber!

Comes with brightly colored burka or somber chador. Beneath, dress her any way you like!

Susan, the White Girl Who Goes After Black Men

Susan hardly eats a thing, so she comes with no tits or ass at all. But she does have a huge case of Jungle Fever! Despite her lack of assets and her inability to dance, Susan has one thing going for her: rich and famous black men want to date her!

Susan is just for show, with straight blonde hair and blue, blue eyes, so don't expect her to engage in any interesting conversations: she is just tooooooo boring and has no sense of humor at all! Like a lot of white folk, Susan is uppity and arrogant without even knowing it. But rest assured that if she's dating one of the brothers, she's probably taking all kinds of abuse that no black woman in her right mind would ever tolerate!

Note: don't let your Susan waste her time running after basketball players. The media may lead us to believe otherwise, but 90% of African-Americans in the N.B.A. are NOT dating or married to Susans.

Sallie Mae, White Trailer Trash

Sallie Mae is dirt poor and was raised in the backseat of a pickup truck, where she listened to country music and learned how to spell important words she would need later in life, like d-i-v-o-r-c-e. Her hair is bleached a perfect white and bouffed to high heaven. All her clothes are skintight, with polyester ruffle trim.

This doll comes with a companion redneck male. Sorry, every one of them happens to be the wrong kinda guy! But we guarantee that Sallie Mae will love him forever. Her removable heart is made to be continually broken and put back together. If she's lucky, no other part of her will get busted! Her ambition is to someday solve her problems on the *Jerry Springer* show. Sallie Mae comes with a falling down trailer and a pretend meal consisting of Spam, chips, Cheez Whiz, and ketchup!

Chapter Seven

THE GUERRILLA GIRLS HAVE HAD A GREAT TIME PUTTING together this guide. We learned things we couldn't have imagined a few years ago, when we began with the idea that stereotypes could be disempowered in Guerrilla Girls fashion, with information and a dose of humor. Here is our short list of discoveries:

Stereotypes
in the 21st century and beyond

First, stereotypes are always in flux. It's amazing to observe how time, specific events, and sometimes individuals have influenced the evolution of a particular stereotype. A Bimbo may be a dumb blonde white girl today, but who knows, maybe someday Bimbo will come to mean a supersmart black female astronaut!

Second, the media has mind-boggling power when it comes to generating new stereotypes (Trophy Wife, Feminazi) and keeping alive the old standards (Prima Donna, Spinster).

Finally, female stereotypes have not begun to catch up with the tremendous changes in women's lives fomented by the liberation movements of the 20th century—civil rights, feminism, and gay rights. So, to help society get with the program, we've designed an anti-stereotype kit to help you fight the unfair and outdated stereotypes you encounter everyday (see next page). Go ape with us! Use the kit on the people around you who try to make you less than you really are. And don't forget to write us at gg@guerrillagirls.com and let us know about the trouble you've made.

Here's another way to be a stereotype buster: turn your Barbies into Guerrilla Girls. Outfits courtesy Jeff. P. Garland

she's young

she's middle-aged

she's old

The Guerrilla Girls' do-it-yourself stereotype eradication kit

Here are some things to help you become a stereotype buster: postcard, button, and T-shirt transfer, for you to xerox, print out, and give out. And that's just the beginning. You can make up your own outrageous anti-stereotype posters and actions. And you can download Guerrilla Girls' posters and stickers from *www.guerrillagirls.com* and put 'em up wherever small minds and lowered expectations lurk. Get busy and don't forget to have fun!

POSTCARD: Send to that special person on the right occasion.

DEAR _____,
IT HAS COME TO OUR ATTENTION
THAT YOU ARE GUILTY OF FEMALE
STEREOTYPING.
_____TELLS
US THAT YOU'VE TREATED HER
LIKE A _____.
KINDLY STOP THIS BEHAVIOR OR
ELSE SUFFER THE CONSEQUENCES.
LEGIONS OF FURIOUS FEMINISTS
ON YOUR CASE IS NOT A PRETTY
PICTURE.

ALL OUR LOVE,
GUERRILLA GIRLS

BUTTON: Wear it and send a guy a message he'll never forget

DON'T STEREOTYPE ME, you redneck, geek, nerd, homey, hunk, pimp, sex addict, hustler, dirty old man, hitman, gigolo, dumb jock, drill sergeant, drag queen, househusband, wimp, OG, serial killer, mob boss, himbo, gansta rapper, lady's man, stud muffin, 98-pound weakling, male chauvinist pig
A message from the
GUERRILLA GIRLS

NOT an
aunt jemima ballbreaker
biker chick bimbo bitch
bombshell bra burner bull dyke
butch call girl carmen miranda china
doll dumb blonde feminazi flapper
geisha girl next door gold digger good
catholic girl harem girl ho homegirl hot
tamale indian princess jewish princess
lady boss lipstick lesbian lolita madam
mother teresa nympho old hag old maid
pinup girl prude rosie the riveter
slut soccer mom squaw stage mom
supermodel tokyo rose tomboy
trophy wife valley girl vamp wicked
stepmother yummy mummy

DON'T STEREOTYPE ME!

A message from the
GUERRILLA GIRLS

Bibliography

Abbott, Elizabeth. *A History of Celibacy.* New York: Scribner, 2000.

Albert, Alexa. *Brothel.* New York: Random House, 2001.

Baldwin, Louis. *Women of Strength: Biographies of 106 Who Have Excelled in Traditionally Male Fields, A.D. 61 to the Present.* Jefferson, North Carolina: McFarland & Company, Inc., 1996.

Basow, Susan A. *Gender Stereotypes and Roles,* Third Edition. Pacific Grove, California: Brooks/Cole Publishing Company, 1992.

Bombshell, Dir. Victor Fleming. Jean Harlow, Lee Tracy. Metro-Goldwyn-Mayer Corp., 1933.

Butch-Femme Network, *www.butch-femme.net*

Butler, Anne M. *Daughters of Joy, Sisters of Mercy: Prostitutes in the American West 1865-90.* University of Illinois Press: Chicago, 1985.

Carter, Alice A. *The Red Rose Girls: An Uncommon Story of Art and Love.* New York: Harry N. Abrams, Inc., Publishers, 2000.

Chapkis, Wendy. *Live Sex Acts—Women Performing Erotic Labor.* New York: Routledge, 1997.

Copacabana. Dir. Alfred E. Green. Groucho Marx, Carmen Miranda. Republic Pictures, 1947.

Corey, Mary, and Victoria Westermark. *Fer Shurr: How to be a Valley Girl, Totally.* Bantam Books: New York, 1982.

Dalzell, Tom. *Flappers 2 Rappers: American Youth Slang.* Springfield, Massachusetts: Merriam-Webster, Inc., 1996.

Encyclopaedia Britannica, Inc., Encyclopaedia Britannica Online, *www.britannica.com/eb*

Faderman, Lillian. *Odd Girls and Twilight Lovers: A History of Lesbian Life in Twentieth-Century America.* New York: Penguin Books, 1992.

—— *To Believe In Women: What Lesbians Have Done for America—A History.* New York: Houghton Mifflin Co., 1999.

Feinberg, Leslie. *Transgender Warriors: Making History from Joan of Arc to RuPaul.* Boston: Beacon Press, 1996.

Flapper. Vol. 1, Nos. 1-7. Chicago, The Flapper Pub. Co., 1922.

Fitzgerald, F. Scott. "Bernice Bobs Her Hair." *Flappers and Philosophers,* 1920.

Fool There Was, A, Dir. Frank Powell. Theda Bara, Edward José. Box Office Attractions, Co., 1915.

Funk and Wagnalls, *www.funkandwagnalls.com*

Garber, Marjorie. *Vested Interests: Cross-Dressing and Cultural Anxiety.* New York: Routledge, 1992.

Gardiner, Mark E. "The Real Wild Ones: The 1947 Hollister Motorcycle Riot" *Classic Bike.* On *www.bikewriter.com/classic_bike.html*

Gentlemen Prefer Blondes, Dir. Howard Hawks. Jane Russell, Marilyn Monroe. 20th Century Fox Film Corp., 1953.

Gilfoyle, Timothy J. *City of Eros: New York City, Prostitution, and the Commercialization of Sex, 1790-1920.* New York & London: W.W. Norton & Company, 1992.

Gil-Montero, Martha. *Brazilian Bombshell: A Biography of Carmen Miranda.* New York: Donald I. Fine, Inc., 1989

Gold Diggers of 1933, Dir. Mervyn LeRoy. Warren William, Joan Blondell. Warner Bros., 1933.

Greer, Germaine. *The Change: Women, Aging, and Menopause.* Books on Tape, Inc., 1992.

Hitchens, Christopher. "Mother Teresa: Saint to the Rich," September 5, 1997. *archive.salon.com/sept97/news/news3.html*

Hotchkiss, Valerie R. *Clothes Make the Man: Female Cross Dressing In Medieval Europe.* New York: Garland Publishing, Inc., 1996.

How to Marry a Millionaire, Dir. Jean Negulesco. Betty Grable, Marilyn Monroe. 20th Century Fox Film Corp., 1953.

Keesey, Pam. *Vamps: An Illustrated History of the Femme Fatale.* San Francisco: Cleis Press, 1997.

Lieb, Sandra R. *Mother of the Blues: A Study of Ma Rainey.* Amherst, Massachusetts: The University of Massachusetts Press, 1981.

Lolita, Dir. Stanley Kubrick. James Mason, Shelley Winters, Sue Lyon. Metro-Goldwyn-Mayer. 1962.

Lord, M.G. *Forever Barbie: The Unauthorized Biography of a Real Doll.* New York: William Morrow and Company, Inc., 1994.

Manring, M.M. *Slave in a Box: The Strange Career of Aunt Jemima.* Charlottesville, Virginia: University Press of Virginia, 1998.

Martin, Linda. *The Way We Wore: Fashion Illustrations of Children's Wear 1870-1970.* Charles Scribner's Sons: New York, 1978.

Mirriam Webster, Inc. Mirriam Webster Thesaurus Online, *www.mirriamwebster.com/cgi-bin/thesaurus*

Nabokov, Vladimir. *Lolita.* New York: Putnam, 1955.

Nagle, Jill, Ed. *Whores and Other Feminists.* New York: Routledge, 1997

National Women's History Project, *www.nwhp.org*

Oxford English Press. Oxford English Dictionary Online, *www.oed.com*

Partridge, Eric. *A Dictionary of Slang and Unconventional English.* New York: Macmillan Publishing, Co., Inc., 1970.

Postman, Andrew. "Athlete of the Century: Babe Didrikson," *Women's Sports and Fitness,* January/February 2000.

Pond, Mimi. *Valley Girls' Guide to Life.* New York: Dell Books, 1982.

Queer by Choice, *www.queerbychoice.com*

Roberts, Diane. *The Myth of Aunt Jemima: Representations of Race and Region.* New York: Routledge, 1994.

Rogers, Mary F. *Barbie Culture.* London: SAGE Publications, 1999.

Rose, Clare. *Children's Clothes.* New York: Drama Book Publishers, 1990.

Rosie the Riveter Trust, *www.rosietheriveter.org*

Shapiro, Laura. *Perfection Salad: Women and Cooking at the Turn of the Century.* New York: The Modern Library, 2001.

Spears, Richard A. *Slang and Euphemism: A Dictionary of Oaths, Curses, Insults, Ethnic Slurs, Sexual Slang and Metaphor, Drug Talk, College Lingo, and Related Matters.* Signet: New York, 1991.

Stenn, David. *Bombshell: The Life and Death of Jean Harlow.* New York: Doubleday, 1993.

"Tokyo Rose," *www.fbi.gov/libref/historic/famcases/rose/rose.htm*

Walker, Alice. "Giving the Party: Aunt Jemima, Mammy and the Goddess Within," *Ms.*, May/June 1994.

Wilson, Dr. Robert A. *Forever Feminine.* New York: M. Evans and Co., Inc., 1968.

Wong, Anna May. "The True Life Story of a Chinese Girl parts 1 & 2." Reprinted from *Pictures*, 1926. *www.thesilentsmajority.com*

Wurtzel, Elizabeth. *Bitch.* New York: Doubleday, 1998.

"The NBA and White Wives," Young African Americans Against Media Stereotypes, July 15, 2002. *www.yaams.org*

Zimet, Jaye. *Strange Sisters: The Art of Lesbian Pulp Fiction 1949-1969.* New York: Viking Studio, 1999.

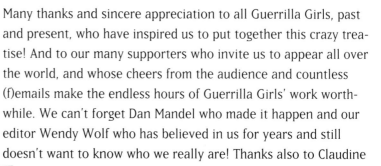

Many thanks and sincere appreciation to all Guerrilla Girls, past and present, who have inspired us to put together this crazy treatise! And to our many supporters who invite us to appear all over the world, and whose cheers from the audience and countless (f)emails make the endless hours of Guerrilla Girls' work worthwhile. We can't forget Dan Mandel who made it happen and our editor Wendy Wolf who has believed in us for years and still doesn't want to know who we really are! Thanks also to Claudine Meredith-Goujon, Dana Rosen, Rachel Harris, Theo Cheng, and Kristine Zaleskas. Many other people have helped us with this book, especially Richard Ross, a true Baboon Boy.

The following individuals deserve special note: Allison Anders, Alice Bach, Tamar Bessinger, the Alice Locases, Cindy Bernard, Amy Bleier, Gabriella Castaneda, Whitney Chadwick, Susie Doolittle, Lillian Faderman, Pam Keesey, Marcia Ann Gillespie, Abby Goldstein, Richard Goldstein, Bianca Grimshaw, Susan Grode, Sarah Jacobsen, M.G. Lord, Robin Morgan, Tom Muller, Jocelyn Nguyen, David Platzker, Nancy Savoca, Ce Scott, Laura Shapiro, Gloria Steinem, Allison Strickland, Noel Sturgeon, Haruko Tanaka, Michelle Taute, Betsey Thomas-Train, Tracy Tynan, Carol Wells and the Center for the Study of Political Graphics, Lynn Zelevansky, and last but far from least: A.L., C.L., and N.W.

We love to hear from all of you out there. The only way to reach us is through *www.guerrillagirls.com* or 532 LaGuardia Place #237, NY, NY 10012. Accept no substitutes!

The Guerrilla Girls have been reinventing the "F" word—feminism—since 1985. What do we do when we're not writing books? More monkey business! We think up new posters, actions, and show up in jungle drag at schools all over the world to provoke others to fight discrimination wherever it lurks.